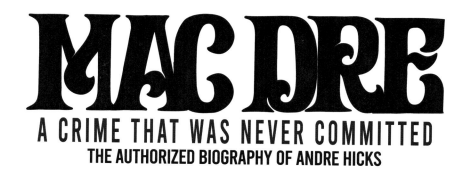

MAC DRE

A CRIME THAT WAS NEVER COMMITTED
THE AUTHORIZED BIOGRAPHY OF ANDRE HICKS

DONALD MORRISON

CONTENTS

FOREWORD
WALTER ZELNICK
PRESIDENT,
CITY HALL RECORDS

first met Mac Dre back in the late 1980s when he came to City Hall Records. I was the rap buyer, and the Bay Area rap market was exploding. He was the tall, young, skinny kid with Khayree who had produced Dre's first releases, *Young Black Brotha*, *California Livin'*, and *What's Really Going On*. I remember Khayree saying, "You gotta distribute Dre's music, man, he's flyin' off the shelves in Vallejo, Richmond, Oakland, we can't keep up with demand." He was right and we kept the stores stocked.

Then Dre caught a phony case and did four years in Lompoc. He was convicted of conspiracy to commit a bank heist that never even happened. He came out with a ton of music pent up inside, and we made a deal to distribute his new Romp Records label. We had great success with his 1996 release, *The Rompalation*, and in 1998 his solo album, *Stupid Doo Doo Dumb*. His fans had missed him during his "hiatus," and snapped up these titles with a voracious appetite for anything new Mac Dre put out. In 2001, we went into business with him in a joint venture: City Hall Records & Mac Dre's new Thizz Entertainment imprint. Over the next three years, we put out about ten Mac Dre albums, and everyone was a hit. And each time he had a new hit, Dre would come into my office to negotiate for more money for production and, of course, for his cut of the action. We would parley back and forth for hours. During one such exhausting session, we took a break, and I noticed the fresh figs on my desk. I had just picked them from the tree in my backyard that morning. I offered one to Dre, and he gave me a look like he was offended by my gift. "Walt," he said with feigned outrage, "a man never offers another man a piece of fruit." I looked at him quizzically for a moment before he broke down laughing, and I did as well, then we both sat down and signed the contract. The result was his two best Thizz Entertainment releases: *Ronald Dregan* and *Genie Of The Lamp*. Both Dre and I were sure that *Genie* would outsell *Ronald Dregan* and we made a "gentleman's bet" with Kilo Curt, who favored Dregan. So far, they're still about even, so no winners.

One day, calls started coming into my office before I arrived. The answering machine was filled with voicemails that ranged the gamut from the inquisitive, "Is this City Halls Records? I heard that Mac Dre was shot last night. Is that right?" One was a matter-of-fact anonymous statement; "Mac Dre is dead." Another was a young girl, weeping, hysterical; "It can't be. I love Dre, my mother loves him, my grandmother loves him, my daughter loves him, my granddaughter dances to his music!" The calls kept coming in all morning. I just couldn't believe it; I'd just seen him a few days ago, and there were no threats he was worried about, and we were about to release his two new albums on the same July date. It was Dre's idea and Mac Dre was the first rapper to do that! I was worried because I couldn't get hold of him, then at noon, the door opened, and Dre walked in with a big smile.

"Yeah, I heard," he said, "But news of my death was greatly exaggerated, Walt." And I thought, 'I've heard that before somewhere.' Then I asked, "Dre, do you know who Mark Twain is?"

"No," he said, "but I know who Mac Yaddadamean is, and he's alive and kickin'. It's all gravy, baby."

Little did I know that a mere three months later, this nightmare scenario would turn out to be real. Mac Dre was murdered. But to all his fans, old and new, he's still alive and kickin' through his music, which will never die.

"They sent me to the pen for five years for a crime that was never committed. I ain't no bank robber but that five years had me thinking maybe I should have did it."

—Mac Dre

CHAPTER ONE
NOVEMBER 1, 2004

At first, she didn't believe it. The mother of legendary Bay Area artist Mac Dre, Wanda "Mac Wanda" Salvatto, had heard rumors about her son's death at least three times before. It came with the territory of being the parent of a larger-than-life rapper, considered Vallejo, California's hometown hero, the founder of Thizz Entertainment, and a key player in the Hyphy movement that still influences hip-hop culture to this day.

But this time, the rumors were true. Mac Dre was gunned down while traveling on a Kansas City highway late on Halloween night in 2004. The fact that Mac Dre was killed thousands of miles away from home at the peak of an artistic resurgence still confounds friends, family, and fans from around the world. It's a wound that's never fully healed. Mac Wanda told SFGATE in the year after his death that she believed Mac Dre had turned over a new leaf—that the saddest part of his passing was that he'd finally separated himself from his former life of crime and had moved to Sacramento to focus on music. He'd even talked of mentoring teenagers to keep them from making some of the mistakes that landed him in prison nearly a decade earlier.

Murals paying homage to Mac Dre can be found across the Bay Area, including one famous installation in the Ivy Hill section of Oakland, California—the place where Andre Hicks was born on July 5, 1970. Every year, there's a celebration on the fallen rapper's birthday christened "Mac Dre Day," that continuously draws thousands of attendees and has featured performances from Bay Area legends like Keak Da Sneak and Andre Nickatina, as well as up-and-comers indebted to Mac Dre's legacy like Nef The Pharaoh and Kamaiyah.

There isn't a single person in the Bay Area over the age of twenty-one who hasn't heard of Mac Dre. He was a certified regional hit before he even graduated high school after gaining radio play, ironically, with a song titled "2 Hard 4 The Fuckin' Radio." He was an artist known for his acerbic wit and raucous storytelling, able to channel the gloomy eccentricities of his birthplace: an area of Northern California known for its gray clouds and counterculture dominance. Mac Dre could have come from nowhere else but the Bay Area, with its colorful palette of windy beach life, party drugs, and dense urban centers that became the playground on which Mac Dre and friends changed the landscape of hip-hop music forever.

Mac Dre's name experienced a resurgence in 2016 after Drake shouted out his name in his wildly popular single "Motto" featuring Lil Wayne. Drake even brought Mac Wanda on stage for his show in Oakland that year. The music video, which has more than 98 million views as of early 2023, opens with a message from Mac Wanda to her son, delivered directly into the camera:

"Andre, you said you wanted me to be a strong Black woman," she says. "If you could see me here now, you'd be proud. I'm still here, and as long as I'm still here, you'll be here. So, don't worry. I got this."

The complete story of how Mac Dre became a regional superstar, the kind of artist whose genius is only fully realized after his death, has never fully been told. Fans of Mac Dre are likely familiar with the highlights, his legendary onslaught of albums, mixtapes, and singles, his role in the Romper Room gang, whom Vallejo police accuse of more than two dozen robberies of mostly pizza stores (a case that was eulogized in a 1992 episode of *America's Most Wanted*), his resurgence after serving a five-year prison bid for conspiracy to rob a bank in the 1990s, and a return marked by a desire to create more positive music in a desperate attempt to finally live happily after a life of setbacks at the hands of a cruel and unfair justice system. But even the most ardent Mac Dre fan doesn't know the full story. It simply hasn't been told yet. Until now.

This is the full story, including a family history, of Andre "Mac Dre" Hicks, told through the voices of his closest friends and family—the people who were there for Mac Dre before he was known as one of the West Coast's premier rap stylists, both in music and fashion, a once-in-a-generation voice that still echoes today.

CHAPTER TWO
MAC WANDA'S STORY

Mac Wanda, née Wanda Wilson, gave birth to Andre Louis Hicks on July 5th, 1970, just one month after completing her junior year at Hogan High School in Vallejo. Mac Wanda is the oldest of her many siblings, including Johnetta, Avis, Cheryl, and John Jr. She remembers her family relying on her in ways that felt burdensome to a young woman and sought to build a life of her own. Her parents, John and Lois Wilson, worked long hours to care for their four kids.

"We had to kinda raise ourselves while they worked," Wanda remembers. "It was a normal neighborhood in Vallejo where we lived. We were left alone a lot; I was the oldest, so I was left in charge. I was so independent—that was some of the reasoning behind me being pregnant with Andre at sixteen."

Wanda remembers her mother being furious at the teenage pregnancy. She was so beside herself, in fact, that Mac Wanda had to put school on pause and leave the house.

"I ended up moving to a girls' home for unwed mothers in Oakland," Mac Wanda says. "In the 1970s, it was devastating for a young girl to be pregnant. I had to leave high school. I was in the eleventh grade when I had Andre."

Wanda finished her senior year of high school while taking care of Andre. She was determined to provide for her son. She picked up a part-time job on Mare Island, a popular peninsula in Vallejo about twenty miles from San Francisco. Even though Mac Wanda worked and cared for young Andre, she still found time to be a member of the Black Student Union and was nominated for homecoming queen, hosting a dazzling waterfront parade complete with polished convertible cars, fellow classmates cheering nearby, and the cool breeze settling in over the bay.

Mac Wanda's parents, the grandparents of Mac Dre, made sure that she felt knowledgeable about and connected to her Mississippi roots. She remembers her family taking long drives to Yazoo City, Mississippi in the summertime to visit family in the Delta.

"I remember it was the country and hot in the summertime," Mac Wanda says. "My grandparents, aunts, and uncles were still there. They had a lot of land with chickens and pigs everywhere. The South was so very different from the North. They made fun of the way we talked when we went down there. They said us Northerners 'talked proper.' Back in the day, the South was very different, but the only place I've ever really known is Northern California."

Wanda's parents were both born in the same exact hospital five years apart; the Afro-American Sons and Daughters Hospital in Yazoo City, Mississippi. John Wilson was born in 1929, and Lois Jackson was born in 1934. Unlike other established Black businesses in the deep Delta South, the hospital was a major safe haven for Black bodies, though only for the few days that small babies were kept within the facilities after arriving. The pride and privilege to find some safety in a brutally anti-Black town and region was vital. Lois lived in Benton, Mississippi at a year old with her father, King Jackson. At this point in 1935, the house was full of energy and hard work. King Jackson, along with his wife Josie, daughters Mariah, Peggy, Charline, Laura Lee, and son James, lived at household number 499, according to the order of visitation from the 1940 census records.

A lot can be gleaned from census records. King was born in 1885 and, as was common in post-slavery Mississippi, worked as a farmer. On just a fourth-grade education, the great grandfather to Andre Hicks, born nearly 100 years later, worked fifty-two weeks per year, instilling a tough work regimen on his children—a trait likely passed on to other kinfolk in the family line. Josie pursued two more years of education before marrying King and becoming a housewife. During that same census visit, nineteen-year-old James Jackson wasn't attending school but had gone as far as fifth grade. He immediately turned to the family business of farming, fifty-two weeks per year, just as his father had done before him. In their district, only 6.21 percent of people had completed elementary school. Laura Lee Jackson was the only child in the family to make it to a seventh-grade level of education. She was married by twenty-five and still living in the sweltering depression (and oppression) of Yazoo City, Mississippi with her parents and siblings.

The blues that most African Americans were fully living during these times in Mississippi gave birth to the actual musical style of the same name. Early blues recordings of the likes of Tommy McClennan's "Cross Cut Saw Blues," and Mary Williams,' "Black Men Blues" depict the harsh realities of life for Black people in the Delta and across the South. The ongoing and ever-growing despair, hurt, and brutality forced upon Blacks in Mississippi continued from generation to generation during slavery and after the Civil War. That blues, which today plays often as quarrels and gripes between lovers and spurned partners, was truly the soundtrack for the greatest aching of the times for Black people: oppression. As a way to rebel, to muster some dignity and worth, Black musical artists recorded field cries, parables, and fables—glorious recordings to honor themselves and their ancestors.

Blues became the first early sign of rebellion and resistance for Blacks in the region, creating new businesspeople and opportunities for Blacks to commune, gather, share stories, and build plans for sustainability. And not all Blacks in Mississippi remained under the thumb of the calculated, cold, white counterpart post-slavery. Eighty miles north of Yazoo City, in 1887, Isaiah Montgomery founded the small community of Mound Bayou, a severely underdeveloped frontier of land. His plan was to attract Black farmers to the area to develop the land and become owners of property, land, housing, and businesses. Less than twenty years later, most of the landowners were Black farmers. Black-owned businesses sprouted up quickly, including a bank, library, bookstore, hospital, and train station. The town produced cotton in massive quantities. Prominent African American leader Booker T. Washington visited Mound Bayou and delivered a rousing speech to locals in its heyday, saying, "It was not the ordinary Negro farmer who was attracted to Mound Bayou colony. It was rather, an earnest and ambitious class prepared to face the hardships of this sort of pioneer work. The scheme was widely advertised among the Negro farmers throughout the state and drew immigrants from all parts of Mississippi, and a certain number from other states."

In the neighboring state, many of the same pitfalls of Southern living fell upon the Hicks family of Mobile, Alabama. Though Allan Louis Hicks, the biological father of Andre Hicks, was born in June of 1952 in Solano, California, his parents Jessie and Dessie had a Southern upbringing. Andre's paternal grandmother, Dessie R.

Hicks née Cooley, was born in 1923 in Mobile and gave birth to her first son Robert just twenty years later in the same city. In 1947, Jessie and Dessie were in love and living on the western edge of town at 1458 Chatague Avenue, surrounded by streets Lafayette, Robbins, Delusser, and Hogan.

In their adult years, the young parents both worked. Jessie worked at a lab not far from their home on Chatague. Perhaps it was the location in which they lived that allowed the Hicks family to hold onto non-laborious jobs. Perhaps it was the size of Mobile in comparison to the Wilson family's positioning in Yazoo City. Either way, life still brought the typical difficulties to Jessie and Dessie, and raising their young son, Robert, in the deep South was a constant cause of contention for the couple. On October 3rd, 1952, four months after the birth of Mac Dre's father Allan, Dessie and Jessie Hicks were united in holy matrimony in Solano County, California, where they had recently become residents.

The late 1940s and 1950s were considered the golden era of train travel. Across the South, thousands of African American youth and their families made the toughest decision of that time period, to leave the Southern states for good. Faced with generational trauma at the hands of their white counterparts, Black families sought refuge, peace, better quality of living, jobs, assets, and resources in major metropolitan cities like Chicago, New York, Washington, and on the West Coast. Western cities like Oakland, San Francisco, and Los Angeles presented huge opportunities for the new generation of Black community members—especially those with military ambitions. There were opportunities to gain higher levels of education, find employment away from labor, farming, and servitude, and expand their reach in the realms of entertainment, art, culture, and community.

Migratory rationales for Blacks were innumerable, but a common theme was the rigor that the journey presented. An often-undiscussed hurt from migration was the separation between generations of loved ones from one another. Not unlike their enslaved elders and ancestors, many African Americans took the blind journey across state lines, through uncharted lands, to escape white persecution. The truth is that the gold rush of opportunities this migration offered promised nothing but hope. So, why did so many African Americans leave the South, while others stayed put? Simply put it was a matter of preferences, relationships, personal interests, businesses—many factors contributed to why some African Americans remained, even through the overarching reach of white oppression.

The journeys for both the Wilson and Hicks families were not easy. John and Lois, childless when they departed the Mississippi Delta, took the California journey to the land of vast opportunities. In Mississippi, the Yazoo and Mississippi Valley Railroad was incorporated in 1882 and began construction in Jackson before continuing into Yazoo City. The railroad was later expanded through the Mississippi Delta and beyond into Memphis. When it was purchased years later, the line was extended to service New Orleans, Louisville, and parts of Texas. Another local rail line was The Yazoo-Delta Railroad, sometimes known as the Yellow Dog. It was opened in August 1897 between Moorhead and Ruleville, Mississippi. It was extended to Tutwiler, Mississippi and Lake Dawson, and was acquired by the Yazoo and Mississippi Railroad by 1903. These lines were later merged around 1946. The most likely method for both families to escape was by train. John and Lois, teenagers living in and through these times, were faced with the same question many generations of Southern-born African Americans faced in the 1940s and 1950s: will you stay?

About 232 miles away, Dessie and Jessie Hicks, with their toddler growing quickly, grappled with the same question. Both families made their journeys, and by fate, landed in the same region of the San Francisco Bay Area. Trains, like every other aspect in Southern society, were segregated. One traveler recalls journeying from less segregated parts of the country into the South as a youth.

"Before crossing into the South, the conductors came through the cars and made all the black folks move to the last car on the train. In Louisville Union Station, there were four restrooms, Men's and Women's, for white and 'colored.' Two restaurants too, for the same reason."

Likely, both the young Hicks family and Wilson family traveled by train, enduring this type of segregation and removal for many days of their trips across multiple trains. Their journeys would likely take between five and ten days, account for nearly 4,000 miles of travel, and consist of many sleepless, mind-wandering days and nights. The journey was likely lonely, wrapped in potentially empty promises. They were leaving behind their parents, uncles and aunts, friends, neighbors, and communities in the hope to find solace in California. What they brought with them were their Southern ideals, family traditions and practices, love for self and each other, and remembrance of their pasts. What they hoped to gain would soon be challenged as they arrived on the West Coast and learned of the ways of the Bay Area in the 1950s and beyond.

Shortly after arriving and settling in the East Bay of Northern California, Lois and John Wilson found viable employment close to home. John had previously joined the United States Navy, and sometime after, Lois took employment at Highland Hospital on East 31st Street in Oakland. John spent many years at the Travis Air Force Base just east of Fairfield, while other servicemen worked at nearby Mare Island Shipyard, which during World War II employed over 50,000 people. Before the war, the region attracted Filipinos who often found work on Navy ships. Early settlers to Solano County brought with them skills as laborers and farmers, many with deep military backgrounds. John would later take up additional work, fixing cars as a side hustle. Just a generation ago, both John and Lois had been born inside the only "colored" facility available to them, thousands of miles away in Mississippi. One of the earliest indicators of the changing times—and perhaps a signal toward better days—was the arrival of their first-born.

Wanda Wilson's birth in the early 1950s symbolized the first family member to be born outside of the constraints of deep south living. Wanda Wilson, the mother of Andre Hicks, was born at Oak Knoll, the naval hospital located in Oakland, California whose primary purpose had been to treat wounded World War II soldiers. Soon after Wanda's birth, a few miles from where John and Lois boarded their train to leave Mississippi, a young Chicago boy named Emmett Till was savagely murdered by white terrorists from the town of Money. It was an early sign to the Wilson family that leaving Mississippi was their saving grace.

Although many institutions on the West Coast were integrated, the military was still segregated. However, the San Francisco Bay Area was home to another form of rebellion and resistance resulting from that very segregated military in 1944. That year, 202 African American Navy men who worked the dangerous job of loading ammunition onto ships lost their lives in an explosion at Port Chicago on July 17th. A year prior, Georgia's sailor district in Vallejo was marred by race riots between Black and white sailors, marines, and civilians. The few Black sailors who survived the deadly explosions were sent to Vallejo's Mare Island Naval Shipyard to continue on with the dangerous job duties of loading ammunition, despite the deaths of colleagues.

At the Vallejo waterfront, many Black sailors refused to continue with the job, despite the impending backlash. The fifty Navy members who refused to work were charged and tried for mutiny by the government at a hearing on Treasure Island. The NAACP and its top attorney, Thurgood Marshall, were put to the task of defending the Black sailors. The court, after a short deliberation, convicted all fifty defendants of mutiny and sentenced them to fifteen years in prison. The men stayed in the Navy after their sentences were reduced, and they were released from prison—but the felony convictions remained on their records.

Wanda grew up in Fairfield in Navy housing that was built in the early 1940s for workers during the war and military families afterwards. When Wanda was still a toddler, John and Lois moved to the nearby city of Vallejo. It was a city still growing, building, and looking for new ways to create commerce, jobs, tourism, and sustainability for its residents. Compared to its neighbors in San Francisco and

Oakland, Vallejo was a tiny town, more rural in city agriculture and climate. The rugged, mountainous terrain, as well as its proximity to the water and to booming San Francisco, made Vallejo an attractive, less infiltrated community for Black and other immigrants coming to Northern California in the forties, fifties, and sixties. The land surrounding Vallejo specifically, had been inhabited by natives for centuries and now more recently flooded with Black soldiers and their wives—some teachers and nurses, some homemakers, some cooks, nannies, and seamstresses.

Black soldiers, their families, and others looking for a new home found a gold rush of their own in small towns like Vallejo and Fairfield. Jobs and housing were a bit more accessible than in the South, and the confining limitations of Jim Crow were not to be found. Vallejo was briefly the capital of California and in the early 1900s, was home to a Class D minor league baseball team. The team was a welcome sight in the small town, a beacon of pride and optimism. The team was referred to as the "Giants" or "The Vallejos." That small-town culture began to breed what some may describe as a "little man's complex" or a "chip on the shoulder" attitude. That attitude would soon give way to musical, sports, and cultural prowess and pride in the region, which became a driving force of joy for Vallejoans.

Wanda grew up in the Bay Area in the 1960s, during a counterculture shift of epic proportions, highlighting the area's most infamous and tumultuous era. The Civil Rights movement was sweeping the nation, and one of its most powerful entities, The Black Panthers, emerged in Oakland in 1966 as a resistance troop to combat police harassment and systematic racism. In neighboring San Francisco, the movement could be seen in the music and art scenes, particularly with the Haight-Ashbury neighborhood's Summer of Love in 1967. There's a small thread to be woven through the flower-power music of the 1960s and the party-fueled, liberating sounds of Mac Dre's later records. You can see the hippie influence in Mac Dre's club drug-fueled anthems—a direct result of his close proximity to one of the most culturally and racially charged areas in America.

Across the nation, art and music depicting the Black rebellion began making waves on mainstream radio stations in ways not possible in the 1950s, when white music executives had Black artists write hits for white singers. "I'm Black and I'm Proud" was released by James Brown in 1968. Black love ballads like "You're All I Need to Get By" from Marvin Gaye and Tammi Terrell and Nina Simone's "Four Women" exemplified America's need for more nuanced interpretations of life in Black America. Sly and the Family Stone, whose lead vocalist attended high school and college in Vallejo, released an anti-prejudice anthem that would eventually become a national hit titled "Everyday People." Vallejo has a rich history of producing talented musicians. Dating back to the early 1930s, vocalist Ivie Marie Anderson reached far beyond local success by becoming the lead voice in legendary jazz impresario, Duke Ellington's band.

A new kind of fear enveloped Vallejo and the greater Bay Area in the final years of the 1960s—The Zodiac Killer's serial murders, seemingly at random, and the subsequent taunting of the media about his crimes. On July 5th, 1969, exactly one year before the birth of Mac Dre, former Hogan High School students Darlene Ferrin and Michael Mageau encountered the Zodiac Killer in the parking lot of Blue Rock Springs Park, less than six miles from where Mac Wanda and her family lived. A man in a tan car approached the couple's vehicle, shooting Ferrin nine times and Mageau four times.

Vallejo police received a phone call soon after in which the male caller stated, "I want to report a murder. If you will go one mile east on Columbus Parkway, you will find kids in a brown car. They were shot with a nine-millimeter Luger. I also killed those kids last year. Goodbye."

It was the second of two incidents that would send a shock-wave of paranoia and fear through the Bay Area. The Zodiac Killer was never officially brought to justice.

In her late teens, Wanda met Allan Hicks, a fellow Vallejo boy whose family had also migrated from the deep south. Allan loved music and was part of a band throughout high school. Mac Wanda was constantly active in current events and social groups in and around Hogan High School. After she graduated, Wanda attended secondary school at Solano Junior College in Fairfield, California. In her early twenties, Wanda secured a full-time job during the day as an administrative assistant in San Francisco, and eventually moved to Oakland because it was easier to commute from the larger city.

"We had cousins there to help me out with Andre as well," Wanda says. "I raised Andre until he was seven or eight in Oakland. When I lived in Oakland, I went to Laney Junior College. Then I met this guy at work named Richard Salvatto. We eventually got married and moved out of Oakland."

Wanda says she lived in Marinwood, and that's where she raised Mac Dre during his most formative years. While working full-time and raising young Andre, Wanda took the long bus ride with the AC transit to go back and forth from San Francisco. She explains her busy life in the early 1970s: "I would drop Andre off at the babysitter, go to the BART station, and go to work. Sometimes I would use BART, but mostly the bus. Even when I moved out to Marinwood, I commuted on the bus. I always had shifts where I could get home in the evening. Of course, I was married when Andre was very young, and my husband would pick him up from daycare. I would come home and do the cooking. I was committed to working and raising my son."

Initially, Wanda worked as a word processor while in school. Later, she worked at Wells Fargo Bank from 6:00 p.m. until midnight.

"As a word processor, you have to remember there was no Wi-Fi or high-speed internet. No technology just yet. We would print out delinquent credit letters. We got graded on how many letters we could crank out. I did that for some years, mostly part-time. I was going to school during the day and working late into the night until my shift changed. Eventually, work at Wells Fargo panned out. I worked there for forty years and retired in 2016."

CHAPTER THREE
WELCOME TO VALLEJO

Music always played an important role in Mac Dre's upbringing. He was raised in an environment that made him eager to become a catalyst for the creation of entirely new musical styles that were so specific to time and place that they would eventually earn their own subgenre—a symbol of their utter uniqueness. Wanda remembers her parents being raised on the blues of the Deep South in the early to mid-twentieth century. When Mac Dre was a young man in the 1980s, disco was emerging as a dominant cultural force, creating a strain of dance music that borrowed the hedonism of the counterculture of the 1960s and infused it with up-tempo dance tracks meant more for clubs than protests. It's a genre that would partially influence Mac Dre in his later years when he began making more party-themed music.

Talented Bay Area musicians of the time included Michael Cooper, who originally founded a music group called Project Soul with friends at Vallejo Senior High School but would later create Con Funk Shun, a legendary band known for their hit song "Spirit of Love." Other artists making waves regionally included Carlos Santana with "Zebop!" and Sly and the Family Stone with "Ain't but the One Way." These were anthems that drove unheralded success for Black Bay Area recording artists at the time.

Wanda and Richard moved Mac Dre to the area he'd forever be associated with in 1980, when he was ten years old.

"We left and bought a home in Vallejo, but not in the Country Club Crest," Wanda recalls of their arrival to Solano County. The Country Club Crest, also known as The Crest, is where Mac Dre would make his bones in both the streets and the rap game. It's situated at the northern edge of town, nearest the Napa County border, cut off from the rest of Vallejo by Highway 37 and Interstate 80. The neighborhood has stayed determinedly African American in a city notable for being one of California's most mixed places, with Latinos, non-Hispanic whites, Asians, and African Americans each comprising at least 20 percent of Vallejo's population.

The Crest's major thoroughfare in the 1970s was Gateway Street. Young kids in The Crest would walk up and down Gateway or drive to the park at the top of the hill and eat free lunch during the summers (a program similar to the free breakfast program started by the Black Panthers).

"People assume that he was raised in The Crest. I wanted to raise Andre differently, so he was raised in East Vallejo. It was an all-white area," Wanda says. "I was determined to live there. For some reason, I always went against the grain. If I wanted to go after something, I went after it. It was a very nice home on the hill. That's where I raised Andre. I was trying to give him a good life."

Andre's younger cousin Dante Wilson, the son of John Wilson Jr., also recalls the evolving, colorful neighborhood where Mac Dre grew into a young man as a predominately white but diverse place.

"East Vallejo had better schools and less crime," Dante says. "South Vallejo was grimy. The Crest was also grimy. Everybody wasn't eating in The Crest back then. But in East Vallejo, you'd rarely see people without a car."

Wanda likes to describe Mac Dre as just a regular kid growing up. He was good, but like most kids, he didn't like to do his chores.

"Was there any chore that Andre liked to do? NO!" Wanda says. "He didn't get a regular allowance. He needed to make up his bed, clean his room, and do the dishes, and just like any other mother of growing kids, I'd be after him to do his chores. 'Do the dishes, Andre,' 'Andre, did you clean that room?'"

Birthdays and holidays were special times for Mac Dre and his family.

"Birthdays we made sure we went to dinner or something. When Andre started making money, he would come around on Mother's Day, Christmas, making sure me and his brother were taken care of."

Mac Dre's cousin Dante remembers Richard Salvatto, Mac Dre's stepdad, playing an important role in his life as a young man. Richard was originally from New York, and he helped expose young Andre to music and culture outside of life in California.

"Big Richard came around early in Dre's life," Dante explains. "He's an Italian guy from New York. Richard was a computer dude back in the 1970s. Dre never wanted for nothing."

Dante remembers Mac Dre always being the flyest at school, dressed in pastels and designer labels even as a teenager. Mac Dre's taste in fashion and access to it gave him an edge in The Crest—an understanding of what the finer things in life actually looked and felt like. Although he rarely used it to flaunt or belittle those around him, Andre instantly stood out among the crowd. Richard was working in an industry very much ahead of its time. Wanda worked full-time in banking. Andre was growing up in places like Marinwood and Eastern Vallejo.

"Big Rich drove foreign cars and Jaguars back then," Dante says. "We learned how to ski early, going on ski trips. They traveled and went to top restaurants. That's what made Dre so unique from the average rapper. He was exposed to a lot more than his peers from The Crest."

Mac Dre grew up in a family-oriented environment with his grandparents, uncle, and aunts nearby. It was a key element that kept him in tune with familial traditions, practices, and music. Wanda remembers that even from a young age, Mac Dre had a magnetism about him that brought family together.

"When he was around, the family wanted to be around," Wanda says. "My house was at the center of it all. My parents, sisters, and brother would come to us. Andre was a part of that. He was a comedian and made people laugh."

Wanda would make recipes passed down to her from her own mother, including her famous gumbo and cornbread dressing.

Mac Dre's aunt on his mother's side, Johnetta Dedrick, raised her son, Carlos, in close proximity to Dre and Wanda.

"They used to ride bikes all over Santa Rosa," Dedrick recalled in the interview after his death, "all up in those hills—Montecito Heights, Howarth Park, Annadel."

Mac Dre began attending Springstowne Middle School in Vallejo in 1983. He went to the same middle school and high school that his mother had gone to all those years before. It was in middle school that Mac Dre would meet a new group of friends and see his social scene slowly branch out. One of Mac Dre's first friends was Dackeia Simmons.

"He gave me his number on the bus on a piece of paper and threw it out the window when I was twelve," Dackeia says with a bolstered laugh. "What do I look like talkin' to skinny ole Andre?" Dackeia says Mac Dre was always a jokester.

Andre and Dackeia shared much in common, including their family's history of migration.

"Our grandparents were a part of the great migration. Mine came from Mississippi, too," Dackeia says. "My father was a Vietnam vet. He worked at Mare Island at the weapon station and built a pipeline in Vallejo. He never got rewarded. They hustled, but back then we didn't even know it was hustling."

Mac Dre's relationship to The Crest began to flourish in his teenage years while attending Hogan High School.

"He gravitated toward The Crest," Wanda says. "He met different kids when they started integrating and busing kids from East Vallejo to school. He started to become friends with kids from The Crest."

One of the first people Mac Dre met was Troy Deon Reddick, known to the world as Da Undadogg, a legendary rapper and producer in his own right. Like Mac Dre, he wasn't originally from The Crest, having been born and raised on Grape Street in the Watts neighborhood of Los Angeles. Mac Dre met a number of other lifelong associates in these early years in The Crest—artists who would come to define the Hyphy sound with him decades later, like Jamal Diggs (J-Diggs), Jamal Rocker (Mac Mall), Major Norton III (Dubee), and Curtis Nelson (Kilo Curt).

Kilo Curt, who's currently a CEO of Thizz Entertainment, remembers meeting Mac Dre for the first time in the summer of 1988 on Leonard Street in The Crest. He says Mac Dre was on furlough from the Boys Ranch, which was a residential community for at-risk children at the time. Kilo's family came to Vallejo by way of Oklahoma in the 1950s.

"My mother was forty-two and my dad was forty-seven when they had me. I was their biological baby, but I was almost like their grandchild, too," Kilo says. He says his birth was a miracle due to his mother's age and that she almost died during the procedure. Kilo remembers existing between two different dichotomies growing up.

"My dad was a preacher, and my brother was a pimp," Kilo says. "Either I was gonna be a deacon of a church or a high roller. I chose to be a high roller."

Kilo recognized Andre's early differences, especially in fashion, from the very first day they met.

"His dress code was mannered and proper. We wore Penn State or North Carolina shit. Black or blue derby. NWA was a big influence. White T-shirts and Nikes. He would wear a sweater. We would say 'damn that shit looks crazy.' That's how we become elite as youngsters though. Niggas would be like, 'damn they fitted.'"

Mac Dre's crew of young hustlers and musicians were christened with a nickname from a neighborhood OG, according to Kilo. The crew became known as the Romper Room, named after an American children's television series, which was franchised and syndicated from 1953 to 1994 and featured a young cast that rotated every few weeks. The Romper Room would eventually be considered a gang by local law enforcement and would be accused of numerous crimes, including bank robbery. But at the time Mac Dre and crew were in high school, it was nothing more than a nickname for a group of fly teenagers looking to make names for themselves.

"We were some young and wild little kids, you know," Kilo says. "He pulled an imaginary magnifying glass like in the Romper Room TV show and called out the street dudes gettin' money, and thus the Romper Room was built." Kilo remembers getting T-shirts made with Romper Room crossed out and Leonard Street Family stitched on in its place. The local kids initially didn't care for the playful nickname, but the name eventually stuck for everyone in the community. Later, in what would be Andre's first hit record, he would embrace the Romper Room name and the humble roots it stems from.

American hip-hop music was experiencing its most creatively rich period yet as Mac Dre finished up at Hogan High School. Artists like Eric B. and Rakim, LL Cool J, and N.W.A introduced new energy, aggression, and seriousness to a genre that was quickly becoming a soundtrack to the gross inequalities of the time. Perhaps no other group was more influential than The Sugarhill Gang, whose mega anthem "Rapper's Delight" eventually sold 14 million records. Mac Dre and his friends would be exposed to other ferocious rap tracks on the radio and soon, on TV, like "How Ya Like Me Now," from Kool Moe Dee and "Public Enemy #1" from Public Enemy. The greatest inspiration for young Mac Dre likely came from Oakland-bred rapper, Too Short, whose album *Don't Stop Rappin'* was released in October of 1983. Not only did Too Short create an album and a label of his own, he lived and recorded his rugged, urban music right in the terrain in which Mac Dre went to school and called home.

Mac Dre was always a fan of different types of music. He didn't just listen to West Coast rap. His stepfather Richard made sure he also listened to rap from the East Coast and other genres as well. While the Romper Room was forming and American hip-hop was transforming, Dackeia remembers going to Con Funk Shun's studio with Mac Dre as kids.

"It was called MELODY'S. It was the recording and production facility where the group's primary California records were recorded. The field trip was great. We grew up to great music around us, and we didn't realize how much it influenced us in different ways. Our teacher, Mathew Smith, was friends with Danny Barker from Con Funk Shun. Foster Hicks was a teacher at Hogan High School in history. He was Andre's uncle."

Mac Dre's interest in music wasn't always paying the bills, though, and he attempted to hold down his first and last job at Burger King while a junior in high school. Wanda remembers the day he got his first paycheck.

"He had a fit when he saw all the taxes and deductions. He was so disappointed," Wanda says. "That's really the only job that he ever had. At sixteen or seventeen, he was already a rapper. He was determined to be a rapper. My whole thing was to push him to finish school and go to college, but he was always determined to be a rapper. He was going to do what he was passionate about."

Vallejo experienced a boom in the mid-1980s after neighboring Oakland and Mountain View lost out on a bid to build a new Marine World/Africa USA theme park in 1986. Before Marine World, the biggest employer in Vallejo was the naval shipyard, which boasted over 10,000 workers. Downtown Vallejo underwent renovations, and more housing was built around the city to help accommodate the new theme park. Today, Marine World has transformed into the current thrill-ride-heavy Six Flags Discovery Kingdom, which is still in operation in 2023.

While Marine World was being constructed, Mac Dre was busy building a makeshift recording studio in his mom's garage. Wanda remembers not being able to park her car inside the garage because Andre and his newfound passion were taking up the space. First came the large rolls of linoleum where Mac Dre and his friends would practice breakdancing. Then he started asking for keyboards in junior high.

"He just picked up a microphone and started rapping,

" Wanda says. "He wrote lyrics as well. When he was fifteen or sixteen, Run DMC and Kurtis Blow were out, and they were his favorites. That's when he decided what he wanted to do. He had a gift of gab, he had a way with words, he was very smart, very young."

This was around the time Andre came up with his stage name, Mac Dre, which pays homage to another one of Vallejo's musical legends, Michael "The Mac" Robinson, who was only able to release two EPs under Strictly Business Records before being shot to death in 1991. Dackeia remembers one summer when she had driver's education classes with both Mac Dre and The Mac.

"We went out driving once and this Asian dude was driving up a hill in Vallejo, and we ended up going backwards down the hill. We were so scared, thinking this kid was about to kill us 'cause he couldn't put the pedal to the metal!"

Mac Dre explained why he chose his stage name in his last interview to be published, recently unearthed by Bay Area legend Andre Nickatina. He said there's different types of Macs out there, and he was kind of a mix of all of them.

"Well, my name happens to be Mac Dre. I got two dozen definitions of that, you know. M-A-C. Master of the Art of Communicating, you know. I got my bachelors in this communicating game. All races, kids. The other M-A-C like Too Short be talkin' about is in the form of a pimp, but he more lenient with his. They structured, they got rules. They get slapped and all that. Mostly a pimp when he talks, he exposes game. He's articulate and can talk and knows more than the average black guy would know. It fascinates these women to be around a real nigga. When they peep the realness, it becomes infatuation. Then most girls who run into money at a young age, eighteen, nineteen, they don't know how to manage they money for nothin' in the world. They can act like they gon' save up to get a Mercedes, but they'll never get that Mercedes. Always got bill problems, so they really are not good financially with handlin' the money. A pimp gon' make sure his bitches is buttered, got money, got cars and everything else, cause the more buttered they are, the better they look, the more the prices go up. It's kinda like a baby on the titty thing, you feel me. You need that titty for a minute. Or some people get strung out on it. So that's my guardian. He can handle my business better than I can. I don't have to worry about bills—he got it all."

The Mac persona from which Mac Dre and his mentor, The Mac, operated was an obvious reference to the 1973 blaxploitation film "The Mack," which was filmed in Oakland and follows the rise and fall of Goldie, played by Max Julien, who returns from a five-year prison sentence and finds that his brother is involved in Black nationalism. Goldie decides to take an alternative path, striving to become the city's biggest pimp. The film's themes and imagery were later duplicated and expanded upon by artists like Too Short and Mac Dre, who embodied the pimp archetype in similar cinematic ways. The film's significant impact on rap culture and on Mac Dre and The Mac specifically can also be seen not only in their choice of stage name, attire, and verbal wordplay, but in their album art visuals where cars, clothes, and women are often displayed.

The center of The Crest's vibrant social scene existed on Leonard Street, where The Mac lived with his grandmother in the 1980s. Also on Leonard Street was Mac Dre's early friend, E.B.

"136 Leonard Street was a trap house, or a dope house, as it was called back then. E.B. had a house at 130 Leonard, so right next to the trap house. He always had it crackin'. His parents didn't want him to do shit. He was acting like he didn't sell dope, but he was on the porch." Kilo Curt remembers. "When the dope game happened, he was in it. He had the long perm, the cars, the money. He was the cool dude. He was a fly dude. A long perm back in the day meant you were the shit. E.B. was one of the money men. He put up studio time, he was like the first CEO of Romp Records until we started robbing to bring the money in."

For a short time before moving to The Crest, Andre lived with John Wilson Jr., his cousin Dante, and family. Dante was in the sixth grade.

"In our family," Dante explains, "all the boys stayed at different houses. Los stayed with Wanda for one year."

People often ask, what attracted Mac Dre to The Crest in the 1980s, when crime was reaching a fever-pitch, and while he had a seemingly nice life in East Vallejo. Wanda explains it like this.

"Andre had a lot of empathy and sympathy for people who struggled. He wanted to help people overcome. For him it came easy. When he met kids in The Crest and he saw the struggle, it affected him. He saw what they didn't have and felt for them. He would give any and everything to them. Things we would buy for him, he would take from our house and give to the kids in The Crest."

Wanda and Mac Dre's stepfather, Richard, provided all the necessities and then some for Mac Dre, but it was his compassion and intrigue with the human experience that caused him to venture into The Crest in search of bonds and companionship that he just didn't have in East Vallejo.

Wanda and Richard, along with Mac Dre and his younger brother Richard Jr., were able to get what they wanted.

"Andre never went without," Wanda continued. "He didn't take advantage, but he was definitely spoiled. I don't know if he gave it away to impress or what. They just didn't have it. It wasn't their world. He was giving. He's known for that. He was giving to a fault."

Later in life, his giving nature arose in a different way, Wanda proclaims. "Him going to prison and not snitching was an example of that. He was willing to give pieces of himself all the time. Andre would see talent and good things in people. He wanted to show them the way and help them make money. He took them with him. Even though some of these guys couldn't rap, he was determined. He shared money with them. A lot of these people didn't realize that he did this out of the kindness of his heart, but HE was the star. They were not. Andre made people feel like they were stars."

Mac Dre's close ties to The Crest continued getting closer through the mid to late 1980s. This caused a certain amount of contention at home, as one can imagine. Wanda says she and Richard bought Mac Dre his first car when he was sixteen years old.

"When he was a teenager, we bought him a car as soon as he was able to get his license. Prior to that, friends would pick him up. A lot of stuff would go on during the day when we were at work. His friends would come to my house, and I wouldn't know it. One day, I came home early from work and my car wasn't there. As I'm coming up the street, here comes Andre in my car. He learned how to take my car. It was a long time before I caught him taking my car during the day. Sometimes he would walk. He was trying to beat me home. He knew my schedule. I was pissed and probably ran out in the middle of the street and had words with him. I used to have to hide my keys. He was in big trouble. That was around the time he switched from being a good kid to a kid who was always getting in trouble. It was a point of contention in my house—those kids in The Crest vs. me. I started to invite the kids to my house to see what Andre was attracted to. Andre didn't wanna be a square, and going to school and attending college was being a square to him. They used to wanna come to my house. They wanted what he had, and he wanted what they had. I started hanging out with his friends, taking them out to eat. That was our way of staying connected to Andre. He moved out to The Crest for a couple years, and that's when he got in trouble: selling drugs, robbing. That's where me and Andre bumped heads."

The first time Mac Dre was arrested was in May 1989 in neighboring Fairfield for giving false information to a peace officer. Kilo Curt recalls a story about a time Mac Dre had his good friend E.B. pretend to be one of his parents so he could be signed out of detention on furlough.

"Wanda didn't even know he was out!" Kilo Curt said.

Even though Mac Dre was spending time in the streets and catching petty offenses, he remained focused on music and wanted to be a professional. He explained in a documentary interview from the late 1990s what the deciding factor was for him to get serious about music.

"I started writing raps when I was seventeen years old," Mac Dre says. "I was in Fountain Springs Boys Ranch doing like six months for joyridin', drivin' without a license, the type of stuff that young playas get into. I started writin' when I was up in there. I came out and started making demo tapes with Studio Tone for $20 an hour in downtown Vallejo. I was just passing the tapes out, and my homeboy The Mac stayed in The Crest on Leonard Street where I'm from. He took my tape to Khayree, and I've been hooked up since then. When Khayree heard it, he said, 'We got to have him on wax.'"

Khayree, whose real name is Khayree Shaheed, would play an important role in the music careers of numerous Bay Area legends, including The Mac, Mac Dre, Mac Mall, and Young Lay. Khayree started his own record label titled Big Bank Records in 1983. He remembers being so broke that he used to cut grass for Felton C. Pilate II of Con Funk Shun for studio time. Khayree says he turned down an opportunity to produce what would become an international hit,

"Rumors" by Timex Social Club. This, along with other setbacks, caused Khayree to have to shut down his record label. However, he eventually found what he was looking for in the form of Bay Area transplant Renald Powers. Renald moved around as a young man, living across the street from San Francisco's notorious Pink Palace in second grade before winding up in Richmond, California for most of his upbringing. Renald grew to be an entrepreneur both in the streets and in the boardroom.

"I owned a GQ Fashions clothing store in Richmond," Renald says. "One day I'm at work doing my thing and a friend of mine was Khayree's cousin. He brought Khayree into the shop, and at first, they wanted to borrow some money for The Mac's new record. His cousin told Khayree I was somebody with some money and I might be interested in giving them some."

Renald says what started out as a quick loan turned into actually being a part of a new record label. He didn't want to just loan Khayree the money. He wanted to invest from the ground up. He already had several successful businesses, including the clothing store, a pager store, and a jewelry store owned by a friend. Khayree was supposed to be a silent partner. He wanted him to make most of the decisions regarding music. Thus, Strictly Business Records was born. It was a record label that gained a considerable amount of attention locally, releasing timeless records like The Mac's certified classic album *The Game Is Thick*. However, Renald says the label struggled financially and never fully became profitable.

"The first few years we were just learning," Renald says. "We used to pay $1 per poster, and we'd press the posters up and just give them away, pressing thousands of posters and sniping them up on billboards. Everything was expensive. We pressed up tapes, pressed up vinyl. We wasted money. Vinyl got played out. Then tapes came out. By the time we did all our promotions, The Mac never got popular. Khayree told me he was going to start another label."

Renald felt that Khayree had used him for his finances and industry connections before immediately deciding to bail when things didn't go as planned. This caused a rift between the two men, as Khayree moved on to start another record label from scratch.

CHAPTER FOUR

TALENT SHOW TO RECORDING STUDIO

Mac Dre was still finishing up at Hogan High School while all this was happening. His friend Dackeia remembers him signing up and preparing for a talent show his senior year.

"We sold See's Candies door-to-door to raise money for the winning prize at that year's talent show," Dackeia says.

She and her classmates eventually raised $7,000, which was certainly a lot of money for high school in 1989. Dackeia remembers it being hot in the school auditorium.

"Hot, like a church needing a fan," she says. "It was steamy, fun, and electric. Andre's song was probably the greatest concert at Hogan High ever, even compared to the Montel Williams event there. I even remember his dancers. Lashonda was one of the background dancers. Michelle Lane and Linda Bryant were dancers too. Everybody knew everybody—Lashonda was from The Crest and rode The Crest bus. And I know The Mac told Khayree to go to Hogan to see his boy Mac Dre do the talent show."

The capacity was 1500 at the talent show, but there were easily more than 1700 people in attendance, including Wanda and Khayree, who watched the auditorium go ballistic during Mac Dre's showcase. The entire crowd knew all the words to Mac Dre's only single at the time, "2 Hard 4 the Fuckin' Radio." He and his dancers won first place, earning the prize money and the adoration of the entire student body at Hogan High School. The grand prize would be the first money Mac Dre ever made from music and would propel him forward into recording and releasing his first EP under Strictly Business Records, titled *Young Black Brotha*. It was mostly recorded at Remix Studios in Oakland and featured "2 Hard 4 the Fuckin Radio" as the first single. But the EP's opening song, the self-titled "Young Black Brotha," speaks more to Mac Dre's lasting influence than the former through its sheer lyricism and revolutionary disposition.

A later friend and collaborator who was connected to Mac Dre's cousin Carlos in Santa Rosa, rapper Ray Luv, had connections to Tupac Shakur. He remembers Tupac actually opening for Mac Dre in 1989 at shows in Marin City. He says Mac Dre had little competition when he was first coming out.

"Mac Dre had very few contemporaries when he dropped," Ray Luv says. "There was no E-40. There was Richie Rich, Too Short in Oakland, Cougnut in Frisco. That was mostly it. I remember me and Tupac got booked to do two shows in Marin City and Vallejo with Mac Dre. Those were his concerts, and that was big for me and Tupac. We were huge Mac Dre fans. Marin City was famous for fist-fighting back then. They weren't shooters like now. All those counties were very close between Marin and Solano, so there was a closeness."

You can see the artistic similarities between Mac Dre and Tupac in their early records, and it's not hard to believe that Tupac borrowed a lot from Mac Dre. Mac Dre's *Young Black Brotha* EP came out two years before Tupac's famous song "Young Black Male." Both songs are very jazzy and ruminating, with themes of black liberation and the inaccessibility of true freedom for the black man in contemporary America.

"Lit lows Daytons and Vogues, a beeper on his belt and a gang of hoes, been in and out of jail since the day he was ten, the hall, the county, and next is the pen," Mac Dre said. This kind of precise storytelling is duplicated in a similar opening for Tupac's "Young Black

Males," an almost foreshadowing for both uprising artists. "I'm tryna effect by kicking the facts, and stacking much mail, I'm packing a gat 'cause cops wanna jack, and fuck going to jail, 'cause I ain't a crook, despite how I look, I don't sell yayo, they judging us brothers like covers on books."

Both Tupac and Mac Dre used the imagery of what they saw and experienced as youth as Black boys struggling to reach adulthood alongside the complications of maturing in the ghetto.

Both The Mac and Mac Dre's early recordings had all the characteristics of hardcore West Coast rap, while retaining a more jazzy and funky sound with an East Coast feel thanks to trendsetting production from Khayree. The Mac's debut, *The Game Is Thick*, is filled with soulful sounds and biting lyrics that provided a real foundation for upcoming rappers in The Crest neighborhood to build off of. On The Mac's second project, the 1990 EP *Enuff of Tis Shit!*, he used heavy samples to make for a new sound in the Bay Area—one which heavily influenced Mac Dre in later years. The album included the song "The Mac," where the nineteen-year-old MC poetically admits, "I'm not sellin' crack." The EP is full of push-the-envelope, controversial material, including a song titled, "Fuck U White Racist America!"

The Mac's anti-crack message is a powerful, bold statement for an MC from The Crest surrounded by peers who indeed were involved in peddling drugs to make ends meet. Using jazzy beats, Malcolm X and Grover Washington samples, live instrumentation, and Khayree's musical leadership, "The Mac" showcases rebellious, youthful energy while captivating with hard, poetic lyrics. The EP's cover art too was influential, as depicted in the art on the debut project by fellow Vallejo rapper E-40 (*Federal*) in November of 1993. In each cover, white law enforcement officers surround Black youth in an attempt to harass and arrest them.

Mac Dre released the follow-up to his *Young Black Brotha* EP in 1991, the *California Livin'* EP, which included some of Mac Dre's biggest songs to date and shows an artist who's clearly not in high school anymore. This was the first EP that Mac Dre released out of school and is pivotal in understanding the arc of his early career. The title track is often considered one of the greatest Mac Dre songs of all time. Much like Tupac followed Mac Dre's lead with the song "Young Black Male," many think he and Dr. Dre did the same thing with "California Love," which shares much in common thematically with "California Livin.'" Other classics from this EP include "Times R Getting Crazy" and "Da Gift 2 Gab." Also on Tupac's album, *All Eyez On Me*, the song "Ain't Hard 2 Find" features Bay Area rapper B-Legit borrowing a Mac Dre line for his verse, saying "I'm from the V-A-L-L-E-J-O / Where sellin' narcotics is all I know," which is origially said on "California Livin.'"

The recording process for "California Livin'" is recalled by Kilo Curt as an important moment in history.

"I remember The Mac was singing 'California Livin' in the corner, just by himself making it up. He was harmonizing and whatnot and Khayree heard him," Kilo Curt says. "The Mac ended up doing all those vocals."

California Livin' went from being a quick demo to a powerful ode to the city that raised both Coolio (who officially appeared on the record and in the credits) and Mac Dre.

Kilo adds, "They took it from a studio in Rancho to Khayree, and Khayree's bathroom is where they re-did the vocals."

With a sped-up sample from Chaka Khan's "Tell Me Something Good" and a crispy, up-tempo delivery on the mic, "California Livin'" gave Mac Dre his first taste of esteem and limelight in the recording business. The video shoot for "California Livin'" was done in various Bay Area locations, including The Crest, San Francisco, Berkeley, Black Hawk (Danville), Los Angeles, and Oakland at Too Short's Dangerous Music Studios.

Kilo says of the impact of the shoot, "Khayree sent a rented limousine for the 'California Livin' video shoot, and that was huge. I was fifteen or sixteen at the time, and my mom was on me about getting a job. So, I said, 'Cuddy, you need a road manager; give me five percent. I had dope money, but I couldn't get a job. If I got a job, they would think I was weak on the streets. You either were in the streets or not. That's how I became Mac Dre's road manager. I started handling business, setting up rental cars. My mom saw me, and she knew I was legit—I was really in the legit game of music with Mac Dre."

Kilo Curt says Mac Dre wanted to sign with Too Short in the early 1990s, but it never materialized.

"We had Strictly Business Records at the time; it was a Vallejo thing, but Too Short was pullin' up in The Crest with 500 Benzes. He had a pool with a dollar sign in it at his house. MC Pooh had just come out with 'Fuckin' With Dank' and had a label and offered us $20,000. We had never had that kinda money all at once, especially not as a check. In-A-Minute Records also wanted to sign us. That's when Khayree stepped in and gave Dre a $30,000 check. That's when my mom started believing in me."

Khayree used financing from Renald Powers, as well as income from producing three records for mainstream pop rapper Vanilla Ice, to fund the multiple-location shoot that was the "California Livin'" video. Of the $72,000 Khayree received from the Vanilla Ice project, he claims nearly $50,000 was used to make "California Livin'" a success. The growth of the Strictly Business label and Mac Dre as a budding rap star widened the eyes of everyone who had a stake to claim in the underground music industry.

It was roughly four years prior to the release of "California Livin'" when Earl "E-40" Stevens and his family group began making music. E-40 also attended high school in Vallejo. In 1986, E-40's cousin B-Legit was accepted to Grambling State University in Louisiana, and E-40 followed, fearing that he would go down a dangerous path without his cousin and confidante. At Grambling, the two became campus celebrities when they won a talent show, creating a rap version of the school's alma mater song, reportedly recorded with future soul star Erykah Badu.

The many connections between Vallejo's sometimes feuding neighborhoods were vast. There was a heightened level of awareness and familiarity between E-40, Mac Dre, Lil Bruce, The Mac, Mac Mall, Dubee, and others. Kilo recalls one of the earliest meetings on a street corner with E-40.

"E-40 pulled up, telling us about his cousin Lil Bruce's song and that he didn't want any problems. 40 played the song, which was dissing The Mac and Mac Dre and a bunch of street factors from The Crest."

The response from Mac Dre and crew was simple; go back to the studio and "sig" back. Sigging, a term popularized in Vallejo, was another version of the tried and true "playing the dozens."

Kilo says, "We went to the studio and made our own. We started siggin!' We would do whatever on those sig tapes. Make a nigga laugh. Hurt niggas' feelings, just going for blood. I'll talk about your dad's grandma. Pissing on graves, crippled grandmas, it was open season."

The infamous "sigging" tapes never saw the light of day and were meant to be more cathartic than actual calls to battle. The "beef" between Mac Dre and E-40 never fully matured, with both artists always seeming to have mutual respect towards one another, even though fan rumors seemed to point in another direction. Mac Dre addressed the feud in an interview with journalist and magazine owner Doxx.

"Ever since I was little, there was tension, right?" Mac Dre said. "I think it started off with one of my homeboys cappin' on one of their homeboys outta The Click. Then it turned into an argument. Then it turned into a boxing match. One person from their side got in, then another person, and it just escalated to high-powered funk for real. Me, The Mac and my homeboy Coolio were representin' on the rap tip for The Crest side. E-40, The Click, and Little Bruce and them were representin' lyrically for their side. It was deeper than the lyrics though."

Dackeia remembers when tides began to turn and relationships began to sour. "Around 1986 and 1987, friends started getting killed. We had a friend named Nate Green who was murdered on his birthday, killed walking home from Marine World. It's sad because Hogan High and Vallejo were such a melting pot of nationalities and people got along well. We had kids who were Filipino, Mexican, Black, White. It was safe."

Mac Dre, now age twenty-one, had a big year in 1991. On June 3rd, his girlfriend, Tara, gave birth to their daughter, Drané Monique Hicks. Mac Dre was excited at the prospect of being a father and was as present as one could hope in those early months. Mac Dre's close friend and mentor, The Mac, was gunned down in Vallejo that year in front of 171 Sawyer Street. Headlines across the Bay Area covered the tragic murder.

An FBI report on the incident gives insight into the shaky street happenings in post-crack urban America. The report states that The Mac was killed in a case of mistaken identity. He and his pregnant girlfriend had been approached while sitting in a car by two convicts who thought they recognized the occupants. The Mac was shot twice in the chest with an AK-47. The two suspects were chased by police but eventually got away. They were both later arrested in Sacramento and charged with the murder of Michael "The Mac" Robinson.

Vallejo and The Crest lost a monumental voice that day—a voice that was unafraid to demand attention with enthusiastic bars, controversial subject matter, and sonically unique compositions. For long-time classmate Dackeia Simmons, she lost hope and a friend.

"The Mac was my buddy. Ah, I just think about him with his fresh Jheri curl, juice everywhere, and us sitting next to each other for a year. Driver's education, all those memories together. He was really a good guy and didn't deserve to die like that."

The Mac's funeral was attended by some of the Bay Area's most promising up-and-coming rappers, producers, and DJs.

"I met Mac Dre at The Mac's funeral," Ray Luv remembers. "Because I went to high school with Carlos, who is Mac Dre's cousin, it was a connection. When Tupac's career took off, I was back on the block with the homies, hustling, doing my thing, and Los pulled up and was like 'why aren't you rapping? You need to be rapping! I said, 'I'm just waiting on my shot.' He said, 'I'm going to introduce you to my cousin.'

"I always wanted to meet these brothas. After the funeral, we were in Crest Park and Mac Dre asked me to rap. When I rapped, he was blown away. He said, 'You dope, I can get you a deal. The next day, I sat in front of Khayree, and two days later, I had money in my pocket and started working on my first project. 'They Don't Understand' was the first song we did that very first studio session and rightfully so, it featured Mac Dre."

CHAPTER FIVE
A MAC NAMED DRE

"In the past six months, twenty-nine restaurants in Vallejo, California have been robbed at gunpoint. Authorities believe that the robberies are the work of a marauding street gang known to operate in Northern California. To date, no innocent bystanders have been seriously injured, but police believe if the holdups continue, violence is inevitable."

—Robert Stack, *Unsolved Mysteries*, March 4, 1992

n the 1990s, urban centers around America were experiencing a sharp rise in violent crime fueled by the crack epidemic. Relationships between a predominately white police force and the Black community continued to deteriorate, culminating in the 1992 Los Angeles riots, set off by the brutal beating of Rodney King, which was captured on camera and played for the nation on nightly news programs. It was the first time that police brutality had been caught on tape and widely viewed by white America. It vindicated the Black community, who'd been complaining of police brutality throughout the history of policing in America.

Music was the dominating force in Mac Dre's life by this point. In just three and a half years, he'd gone from a break-dancing kid to a high school rap phenom, then a formidable hip-hop underground star in Northern California and even beyond. With his 1992 album *What's Really Goin' On,* a frustrated Mac Dre balances emotions of anger and loss at the death of his comrade The Mac with major resentment toward local law enforcement and the judicial system as a whole. On the title track of the album, he unleashes a somewhat satirical "Jack and Jill" story that crosses from fairytale to harsh reality—one that becomes strikingly similar to his own story, in which he raps:

"Little Jack Junior grew up to be fly.

A shake 'em, break 'em, take 'em player kind of a guy.

When others would grind, Jack Junior would rhyme.

I guess to this fact, the rollers were blind.

He had dreams of rappin', gold and platinum.

But rollers would jack him, and steady attack him.

One day they beat him down, hit him all in his crown.

He swung and hit one, they sent him to the ground.

Cuffed and stuffed him, continued to rough him.

In jail they stuffed him, when Jack did nothing.

Charged him with assault on a C-O-P

Tryna stop him from getting to the T-O-P

Had a max of four, pleaded and got two.

Now he's in jail on a deal he copped to.

Thinkin' 'bout the day when he gets home.

Huh, what's really going on?"

The January release of *What's Really Goin On?* also included a remix of "California Livin." Perhaps no better song demonstrated Mac Dre's frustration with Vallejo police than the standout track, "Punk Police." His charge against them was easily warranted, as his brief run-ins became more frequent before and after the release of "Punk Police." His own animosity stemmed from personal issues with police harassment of himself and his friends in the neighborhood and elsewhere. He was arrested or received citations in Fairfield and Vallejo for everything from making terrorist threats to assault on six different occasions between 1990 and 1991. Mac Dre was intent on letting local officials and fans know that his friends were not a gang, as they had consistently been labeled in newspapers by officers.

"You labeled us a ruthless G-A-N-G, but the biggest gangsters are on the VPD," Mac Dre says in "Punk Police."

Unknowingly and without radio or video support, Mac Dre became a marked man under law enforcement's gaze and also a spokesman for his community, and not just another street rapper to glorify the mackin' that he had become known for at this career junction. A police log of the activities of Mac Dre and his friends, including constant street surveillance, shows a persistent attempt by officers to catch the group of teens and young adults slipping in the early 1990s. The surveillance began years before Mac Dre ever faced any real time behind bars. Not only were Vallejo police investigating, following, and harassing Mac Dre by early 1990, but when the Romper Room game began to become synonymous with criminal activity (including bank robberies), the FBI got involved.

Early Mac Dre funding source and executive producer Renald Powers contests the bank robberies that the Romper Room gang were being accused of at the time.

He says, "Ain't nobody out there besides his mother who can say they took money out of their pocket and paid for him to get on, besides me and Khayree. I'm talking about real money. They say they were robbing banks and giving it to Mac Dre? They weren't doin' that."

Since his release from prison, close Mac Dre associate and co-defendant J. Diggs has been open about his personal involvement in the bank-robbing enterprise. He admitted recently in a VLADTV interview that the crew was responsible for taking down nearly fifty banking institutions and pizza parlors, all the while, frankly, stating that Mac Dre was never involved. Diggs articulated that the robberies would be conducted in "takeover style," where the robbers would quickly enter, secure any patrons and employees, demand money, and leave quickly. Diggs has gone on to say that everything was always done in the same fashion—quick and methodical.

According to Diggs, they all knew they were being watched, and they were being stopped constantly. Ironically, after one bank robbery in San Francisco where Mac Dre's mother Wanda was presently working, her son received a frantic call.

"The FBI came in, showed us photos," Wanda said. "I called Andre immediately. I was terrified and pissed. They were pointing guns at us, demanding money. I asked him if he was a part of it, and by his answer, I knew for sure he wasn't."

The Hollywood film industry has often glorified and romanticized the idea of robbing banks, from Westerns and 1950s films about train heists to modern-day cinema that seemingly celebrates it. On August 16th, 1991, the Bank of America in Livermore, California was targeted for a bank robbery. The details of the crime were later broadcast, giving general descriptions of suspects.

"Before 10:00 a.m., one suspect who is five-foot, five and another six foot one and muscular enter the bank. They are, in total, five fully clothed and masked males. They enter the bank and immediately fire four rounds from a 9-mm type Uzi weapon into the ceiling. 'This ain't no joke. This is a robber,' one shouts. Two or three jump the teller counter into the teller windows that are open for business. At least one of the containers was brought with them. Robbers are somewhat physical with all three females during the robbery, and the fifth man stays in the teller area. Robbers in masks but appear to be Black based on their diction."

After that robbery, the supercharged FBI surveillance of Mac Dre and anyone else associated with The Crest or the Romper Room gang was in full force. By September seventh, a report was circulating between governing parties in law enforcement and included the use of a confidential informant—also referred to as a snitch—who was later revealed to be Corey Dunn. Corey was gunned down in 2010 on Woodrow Avenue in Vallejo, nearly thirty years after helping to send his former friends to prison.

A huge break into the pizza and bank takeovers came when TV show producers for *Unsolved Mysteries* got involved. The *Unsolved Mysteries* segment on Romper Room aired on March 4, 1992—the same month in which Mac Dre's *What's Really Goin' On?* was released. The episode featured Vallejo detective Rick Nichelman and Dana Meyers, a pizza parlor supervisor.

Nichelman was quoted during the episode, saying, "Some of the language they've used during the commission of these has been very specific, like 'Don't make this a 187,' which in California is the penal code section for murder."

The show's host, Robert Stack, says in the episode that, "the robbers seem familiar with the layout of each individual target and go about their business with brisk, cold efficiency. Within minutes, the thieves have vanished, leaving police with almost no clues and a handful of terrified victims."

Wide coverage of the bank robberies and pizza parlor break-ins flooded local news after the arrest of the supposed perpetrators in March of 1992. The harassment of Mac Dre and his friends was very real. Mac Dre was followed and eventually arrested in Fresno along with Kilo Curt and J. Diggs.

On that day, he'd decided to hitch a ride to Fresno with Curt and Diggs so he could meet up with a girl he'd met while performing a show two weeks earlier. On the way back to Fresno, the car was pulled over and surrounded by officers from the Federal Bureau of Investigation as well as Vallejo police.

The police say that while Mac Dre was getting busy in a local motel with his lady friend, his accomplices were out casing a Fresno bank with plans for a robbery. But a local news crew had caught wind of the robbery over the police scanner and had prematurely gone to the bank. When Mac Dre's friends saw the news crew, they called it off, according to documents provided by the FBI.

However, police still felt they had enough evidence to pull Mac Dre and his friends over and charge the crew with conspiracy to commit bank robbery.

In a scene recounted by J. Diggs in the *Legend of the Bay* documentary, Mac Dre actually noticed that the men were being followed by an undercover cop before police attempted to pull them over.

"We were on the highway heading north, back to the Bay Area," J. Diggs says. "A car passed by. Now, I'm sitting in the driver seat, and I'm facing Mac Dre. On his face, it looked like he'd seen a ghost. Something was not right. I wasn't feeling it."

J. Diggs continues: "So what I did—instead of going straight on the freeway, I smashed across the intersection of the freeway, across the median, and started driving the other way. When I did that, it looked like every car on the freeway did. There were about thirty

FBIs. They were following me, and they all started peeling off the freeway. That's when we realized they were on to us."

FBI case files released years after the trial reveal the extraordinary lengths authorities went to in order to catch the alleged bank robbers. Surveillance units present that day included FBI Special Agents, Fresno County Sheriff's Office deputies, Fresno Police Department officers, and Vallejo Police Department officers. By this point, Mac Dre had attracted the ire of local and federal law enforcement with lyrical taunts that police believed were being funded with capital gained through the pizza shop robberies and credit union stick-ups. Although, by all accounts, including J. Diggs' autobiography, Mac Dre never took part in any robberies. He was merely the artist that his crew rallied behind in an attempt to use their spoils for something that had real meaning. Mac Dre's music had the momentum and potential to change the financial lives of the entire Romper Room crew. Members who grew up engulfed in poverty and forced to commit crimes to get a leg up in the music industry now saw a way out through Mac Dre's artistic vision.

According to the surveillance log, the men were riding in a champagne 1991 Chevrolet Geo, rented recently at a Budget Rent-A-Car in Vallejo. The FBI files include a list of items confiscated after the group was pulled over.

"White cotton ball cap with UNIVERSITY OF NORTH CAROLINA on it.

Sony portable stereo, model CFS 720.

Electric cord for a stereo.

Light blue Levi jeans.

White T-shirt.

Pair of dark blue cotton gloves.

One pair of gray cotton gloves.

Two cassette tapes, a Sony and a TDK.

Red spiral notebook.

Black Page Net Motorola pager.

BUDGET RENT-A-CAR rental agreement.

Pair of Nike tennis shoes with gray tape around them size 7.5.

Glock 9mm semiautomatic handgun, serial number with a clip.

"Aspen" deodorant and aftershave.

Copy of the Vallejo Times/Herald, dated Wednesday,

March 25, 1992.

One roll of gray duct tape.

Receipt from FOOTLOCKER, dated 3/25/92.

Packet of Zig Zag papers.

Two Nike shoe boxes."

The police also found two black ski masks about forty feet away from where the group stopped, with the belief that the crew had tossed them from the car after noticing police attempting to pull them over.

"Each ski mask has a sewn logo on it, which is circular, and bears the logo of the Washington Redskins," according to the FBI files.

The trial turned into a circus almost immediately. A local news report included in the FBI Files reported that "the normally somber federal courtroom of Judge Robert Coyle pulsed to a rap beat," during parts of the trial. Prosecutors played portions of "Back N da Hood" as part of their effort to show Mac Dre's connection to the Fresno bank robbery. "The bank was robbed, and I fit the description," Mac Dre raps on the song. They also played for the jury lyrics like "Man, you can't even find who's been robbin' you blind. You had to blame somebody . . . so you're going to frame somebody," from *Punk Police.*

Mac Dre's lawyer, C. Don Clay of Oakland, argued in the U.S. District Court that his client had been targeted by authorities simply because of the anti-police messages in his early music. But to the police, it didn't matter whether Mac Dre was actually committing the robberies. In their eyes, he was still profiting off the cash stolen, and when they caught him slipping in the Chevrolet Geo with J. Diggs and Kilo Curt, they seized on the moment to hem him up. It's why the judge eventually handed him the maximum penalty for conspiracy to commit bank robbery and why he did nearly the entire stretch of his five-year bid.

According to J. Diggs in his book, *Soul of a Gangsta*, Mac Dre used his time awaiting trial calling radio DJ's and giving exclusive interviews. One of those DJ's was Mr. Marshall on a syndicated radio show called *Street Soldier.* During one call, Mac Dre told the world that he, Kilo Curt and J. Diggs were all innocent, and blamed everything on the driver that day, Corey Dunn. J. Diggs said that the feds immediately went to Mr. Marshall and ordered him to stop interviewing inmates. But the damage was done. The entire Bay Area now knew what Dunn had done that day in Fresno. He'd worn a wire and entrapped his close friends to avoid spending time in jail on another charge. Mac Dre outing Dunn and managing to have a voice during the early days of the trial solidified his reputation in the street and furnished him with a cult following in the Bay Area. His album released from behind bars with Khayree also showed fans his commitment to the art form.

Mac Dre was sentenced to five years for refusing to accept a plea deal. His accomplices were convicted of attempted bank robbery and given ten years. This all happened just eight days after Mac Dre released the *What's Really Goin' On?* EP and only weeks removed from opening for West Coast legend, Ice Cube, at a show. What should and could have been a superb launching pad for Mac Dre's career turned out to be a four-year and four-month nightmare for the young MC.

The police in the Bay Area must have been pretty confused when the local robberies of banks and credit unions continued unabated even after J. Diggs, Kilo Curt and Mac Dre were all sentenced for the attempted robbery in Fresno. Robberies were still taking place at a breakneck speed and eventually, while all three men were still serving time in federal prison, the police would make their move against what was left of the Romper Room gang.

In April 1998, Vallejo police, agents from the state Department of Justice and the FBI, arrested fifty-three members and associates of the Romper Room gang after a yearlong investigation. They were accused of taking more than $1.5 million in the past two years from banks and credit unions in San Jose, Santa Clara, Sacramento, Stockton and Vallejo. The detectives also alleged that the group went further by bragging about their crimes, specifically the robbing of credit unions, on the song "Uninvited" off *Mac Dre Presents the*

Rompalation. A Vallejo Police Department press release stated that Mac Dre was one of the suspects rapping about the robberies, but if you look closely at the lyrics of the final verse, he was the only rapper on the track who wasn't rapping about robberies.

However, those facts didn't matter and the song itself was paraded around by local police as one of the reasons more than two dozen men were arrested for the string of robberies. It would seem that the cowboy image portrayed by Mac Dre, Kilo Curt and J. Diggs inspired scores of young people in the Bay Area to attempt to commit the same crimes they saw their heroes taking part in. As J. Diggs described it in his book, Vallejo gangsters were becoming known for their affinity for bank robbing and their exceptional talents at being able to escape unscathed for years.

"Robbing banks was what our neighborhood became known for. Niggas in the Crest felt like that was what we did; we robbed banks, and they went crazy with it," J. Diggs said. "The bank robberies got so intense and overwhelming that the feds went and swept up the entire hood. They picked up a total of fifty-two people. As soon as they grabbed them, they immediately associated them with us—the Romper Room Crew. Because the robberies were of similar styles and they were from our hood, the media made it seem as if we were the masterminds behind everything. It had nothing to do with the Romper Room Crew, though; it was just a new generation that had clung on to something we had started."

CHAPTER SIX
THE THIRD-GENERATION MAC

t was during the trial that Khayree began to focus his attention on another artist.

Mac Mall has referred to himself in interviews as the "third-generation Mac," following Michael "The Mac" Robinson and Mac Dre himself. Mac Mall even had the opportunity of collaborating with Mac Dre for a full-length album, *Da U.S. Open*, released posthumously less than a year after his death. The album is a high point in both artists respective discographies and showcases the two's natural chemistry and unassailable wit. But before Mac Mall and Mac Dre reunited for *Da U.S. Open* in 2004, their relationship had gone through numerous phases, with the two not speaking for a number of years.

Mac Mall's family comes from a similar background as Mac Wanda's. They, too, came to Northern California from the deep south, according to Mac Mall in his autobiographical book *My Opinion*.

"My grandmother, Big Momma, loves to talk about how she used to work from sundown to sundown when she was young, you know, in the field, picking cotton," Mac Mall said. "Sometimes she picked a couple of hundred pounds a day for pennies. One of the reasons she was interested in my grandfather, Big Daddy, was that he didn't pick cotton; he cut puck-wood trees."

Mac Mall's father was in the U.S. Navy and the family traveled around the country when he was young. He even lived for a couple of years in Alaska before finally settling down with his family in the Country Club Crest. He describes hip-hop music as his one true love. The first rap song Mac Mall really loved was "The Message" by Grandmaster Flash.

"Whenever I heard it, I would get a warm feeling in my chest that would get hotter and hotter until I couldn't help but rap the verses word for word," Mac Mall said. "Some people say they feel this way when they fall in love for the first time. Well, I believe them, 'cause when I was introduced to hip-hop and rap, I knew that it would be my first and only true love."

The first tapes he remembers getting were a gift from his grandmother on his father's side. Records from artists like Whodini and Fugitive and Run DMC's "Rock Box." Later he was put on to local legends like Too Short, who was at that time the biggest hip-hop artist from the area. Too Short's pimp-like musings personified the Bay Area in the late 1980s and early 1990s. He also lists local Bay Area artists Magic Mike and Calvin T from Richmond as early inspirations as well. Both Magic Mike and Calvin T are considered early architects of the type of pimping-inspired raps the Bay Area would become known for. But more than anyone else, it was Michael "The Mac" Robinson that Mac Mall looked up too.

"Some fools thought Jordan was dope, but the only Mike I wanted to be like was The Mac," Mac Mall said. "I remember The Mac from back in the day. He lived on Leonard Street. He was always into music, and I used to see him riding a moped with speakers on it. Plus, he was always rappin'. But back then when I was introduced to him, he had come all the way up."

It was through The Mac that Mac Mall would come to know Vallejo's hottest producer at the time, Khayree. Mac Mall says Khayree first heard him rap on a four-song demo produced by Mac Dre.

Mac Mall was only fifteen years old when he recorded a four-track EP, produced by Mac Dre, which ended up catching the ears of Khayree. Mac Mall was invited to the studio to rap for the hottest producer in Vallejo, who ended up playing him the beat for what would eventually become the title track of Mac Mall breakout debut album, *Illegal Business?*, released in 1993. It wasn't easy convincing Mac Mall's parents to let their teenage son pursue the life of a rapper before graduating high school. Khayree and another associate, Ceese, had to go to Mac Mall's parents' home and vouch for Mac Mall's natural talent and his potential as a recording artist.

"After Khayree finished his presentation, Ceese assured my parents that he would look out for me as best as he could, acting as DJ/mentor," Mac Mall recalled. "After Ceese and Khayree bounced, my parents let me know that they thought I shouldn't risk my future on a dream and that I should concentrate on school. Then they informed me that if I disobeyed them and chose a music career, I would be doing so alone and without their support."

Mac Mall decided that his prospects at life with Khayree and Ceese in the music industry were just as appealing, if not more, than sticking around Hogan High School and smoking weed with his friends. He figured capturing the momentum he already had with his music was a risk worth taking, with or without his parents' support. However, he convinced his mom to sign the contract and Mac Mall became the first artist ever signed to Young Black Brotha Records. With Mac Dre getting ready to serve half a decade in federal prison, and The Mac's untimely passing a few years earlier, Mac Mall was primed to become the heir to the musical foundation set by his legendary mentors, years before. Khayree pivoted as well and began focusing all his attention on Mac Mall.

But Mac Mall wasn't the only one holding Mac Dre's name down while he was serving time. He remembers Ray Luv's single "Get My Money On," as a regional hit and certified classic. That single was from Ray Luv's *Who Can Be Trusted?* EP. He also worked on remixes with Janet Jackson and En Vogue. Also in the mix was E-40, who became perhaps, the biggest artist in the Bay after Mac Dre during this time. Mac Mall remembers meeting Tupac Shakur on the set of E-40's video for "Practice Lookin' Hard."

"Pac was there with Mopreme, Stretch, Big Syke, and a couple of his folks from the Bay," Mac Mall said. "He looked like success; at the time, he was on his way to becoming the biggest rap star alive, and the best thing about it was that he was from the Bay."

Tupac would go on to direct Mac Mall's video for "Ghetto Theme," off of *Illegal Business?*, showing the ghost of Mac Mall haunting the man who shot him over a disagreement during a dice game. It's one of the best rap videos of the 1990s and correctly conveys the helplessness of street violence from multiple perspectives. The video was shot in Los Angeles and Mac Mall says in his book that Tupac decided to shoot another video for Ray Luv that day, for his single "Last Night."

"Tupac was a godsend," Mac Mall remembers. "This was the first time he had directed and was doing two videos in one day. He made the treatment, picked the film crew and basically ran the show. He was doing all this while he had cases in almost every state, but yet you could never tell by looking at him."

Illegal Business? is considered one of the most important gangster rap albums of the 1990s. It shows Khayree homing in on the sound he'd begun crafting with Mac Dre years earlier. In a post-*Chronic* world, Khayree upped his game and began competing with Dr. Dre, who was the most innovative beatmaker coming out of California at the time. Khayree's soundscape on *Illegal Business?* utilized the synthesizer in ways that weren't being done at the time, and perhaps wouldn't be repeated until Kanye West emerged from Chicago in the early 2000s. Mac Mall's young age made him stand out from other rappers at the time, and added a youthful authenticity to his raps about gang violence, pimping and hustling to survive. For such a young man, Mac Mall's lyrics were able to contain real perspective. He wasn't merely glorifying his dangerous lifestyle, he was reflecting on it with the wisdom and care of an old man, all before he could legally buy a pack of cigarettes.

Mac Mall remembers when Tupac invited him to the Soul Train awards in 1993, he was so young that he had to get his mom's permission to go. Tupac himself called the young rapper's mother to get her blessings.

"He couldn't have called at a worse time, 'cause I wasn't doing well in school," Mac Mall remembers. "When he asked her, she straight up told him 'no.' I almost fainted. I had to explain to her that this was a once-in-a-lifetime opportunity, and I had to get out there. Luckily, I was able to get my grades together and go."

Mac Mall quickly signed a deal with Relativity Records in 1996. They pulled out all the stops for his sophomore album, *Untouchable*. The album included singles "Get Right" featuring Levitti and "Let's

Get a Telly." According to Mac Mall, the corporate overlords at Relativity didn't put the time or energy into making his *Untouchable* as big as it could have been. Disputes erupted over Mac Mall's contract and Relativity even blocked him from doing features for a time. Mac Mall, never one to be intimidated, went against their orders and appeared on *Mac Dre Presents the Rompalation* that same year.

It was around this time that Khayree would branch off on his own and release one of the most pivotal records of his career. His debut album, *The Blackalation*, came out in 1997 and featured head-turning appearances by Mac Dre, Ray Luv, Big Syke of Thug Life and Dubee, among others. It included some of Mac Dre's first solo songs recorded after his first release from prison, aside from tracks included on Dubee's self-titled album and on Master P's *West Coast Bad Boyz II*. Khayree's official debut holds a cohesion usually missing on producer-led albums. Each song blends into the other, creating a dizzying trip through the Bay Area's most notorious hoods. It also features a supporting cast of the area's most promising rappers at the time and includes two certified Mac Dre classics, with "Back 2 My Mission" and "Livin' That Life." It showed that Khayree could put together a complete album with foresight and skill, making him one of the most sought-after producers in the Bay Area.

At the same time, the third-generation Mac was slowly becoming disillusioned by the music industry. Mac Mall traveled around the country and worked with some of the biggest names in hip hop, and yet still found himself back in the Bay Area attempting to make ends meet. Mac Mall reports that he began pimping around this time in order to make money when he wasn't working on new music. Thankfully, Khayree linked back up with Mac Mall in 1999 to release a collection of songs they'd begun working on years ago during the original *Illegal Business?* sessions. The follow-up was called *Illegal Business 2000* and would go on to feature perhaps Mac Mall's biggest song ever, "Wide Open," a lady's anthem with smooth production centered around a head-nodding piano. The song finds Mac Mall at the height of his pimping capabilities, easily speaking the language of lust and love over some of Khayree's most inspired productions of his career.

Mac Mall spent the next couple years moving around the Bay Area, Los Angeles and Las Vegas. It wasn't until a party celebrating J. Diggs' release from federal prison that Mac Mall would be summoned back into the music industry. The party took place on a cruise ship circling the Bay Area and was attended by numerous Bay Area luminaries, including J. Diggs' original co-defendants, Mac Dre and Kilo Curt. According to Mac Mall's book, it was at this party that Mac Mall and Mac Dre's minor beef finally came to an end, with J. Diggs and Kilo Curt orchestrating the meeting of minds.

"When he first told me about the idea, I was like, 'Fuck that,'" Mac Mall said. "But Diggs and a couple of turf OGs were able to convince me to consider it. The main reason I came to the table to squash the drama was that Mac Dre and I, regardless of whether we liked it or not, were connected. We were the two figureheads of the Country Club Crest, and our turf was the womb that bore many boss macks. The fact is that we couldn't let our personal differences fuck up the main goal, which was to represent the Triple Cs for the world to see."

Both Mac Mall and Mac Dre successfully settled their beef and even christened the moment by performing at the party together, just as they used to do Crestside hood parties more than a decade earlier. It was at the J. Diggs release party that Mac Mall would also get reconnected with Khayree and Ray Luv, who was finishing putting out his own record, *A Prince in Exile*, on Sessed Out Records. The two Macs also officially laid out the plans for their collaborative project, *Da U.S. Open*, which would unfortunately not be released until after Mac Dre's death in 2004.

Mac Mall and Khayree officially put their creative rekindling to good use with *Mackin Speaks Louder Than Words*, which featured appearances from Big Syke and Sleep Dank. This album would see Mac Mall attempting to have a little more fun with his music, while still keeping his ruthless and pimp-like edge. On "5-3-5 (Five-Tre-Five)," Khayree sampled "Something for Nothing" by MFSB from their self-titled album, a year before Jay-Z would do the same thing for his song "What More Can I Say," off *The Black Album*. This shows Khayree's ability to be ahead of his time when it came to producing records.

Mac Mall has more than earned his place in the rap hall of fame. He's sort of like the Forrest Gump of Bay Area rap: he participated in every important era, from hanging out with The Mac, Mac Dre and Tupac, to recording with Khayree and E-40. His music was able to translate what it felt like growing up in the Bay Area more succinctly than almost anyone else. His relationship with Bay Area OGs has never faltered, and after Mac Dre passed, his bond with what remained of Thizz Entertainment only grew stronger.

CHAPTER SEVEN
SILKY SLIM

Upon their detainment, Mac Dre, Kilo Curt, and J. Diggs were separated and interviewed. The police interview for Kilo Curt was unsuccessful.

When he was asked repeatedly whether he was to be a primary part of the robbery, he stated, "I can't say anything about that. I got nothing to say," according to FBI files.

Mac Dre's interview with investigators took place at approximately 3:03 p.m. According to police files, he was wearing, "a white T-shirt with blue printing and the words Mac Dre on it; white pants (believed to be sweat pants) with white pants underneath; white socks and white NIKE tennis shoes; gold hoop earring in right ear; with a physical description of six-foot-one, 135 lbs., black hair, brown eyes, and a mustache and beard."

Billy Jam, hip hop historian and radio broadcaster, was a witness at the trial on Mac Dre's behalf and recalls his early interactions with the budding megastar.

"We've been tight since day one. I knew Khayree and The Mac and then Mac Dre came along. We had him on my radio show before and after he put out records. I always interviewed him on radio and for articles. I knew his mom. Mac Dre came on my radio show after The Mac was killed and was talking about it. He was a really cool guy."

In their original pursuit to nab Mac Dre and anyone affiliated with the Romper Room Gang, the FBI and local agencies compiled over 1,120 pages of documents, classified as surveillance, to solidify a case against them. The coverage of Mac Dre's arrest was widespread, not only in the Bay Area but across the state of California, including in the *LA Times* and *San Francisco Examiner*. Days after his imprisonment, a story also appeared in Chicago's *JET Magazine* referring to the rapper's trouble with the law. In some ways, his arrest increased his profile on the national stage, particularly during a time when some rappers' street credibility came into question.

Mac Dre never lost touch with Khayree and began recording an album in secret over the Fresno County jail phone lines. It's an artistic achievement to remain creative while behind prison bars; it's an environment designed to sap inmates of any will to live, much less create art and poetry. Mac Dre was one of the first rappers unfairly targeted and prosecuted for crimes they never committed. Prosecutors used lyrics from the *Young Black Brotha* EP to help establish guilt in his case. While still incarcerated, Mac Dre re-released *Young Black Brotha* as his debut album in 1993, featuring a number of songs with vocals recorded through a jail phone.

He also released an EP titled *Back n Da Hood,* which used recordings from his time in Fresno County jail. *Back n Da Hood* included the title track plus deep cuts like "93," "Love Dat Donkey," "It Don't Stop," and "My Chevy," which officially opened the door for third-generation Vallejo "Mac" rapper Mac Mall, just seventeen at the time. Mac Mall unleashed a flurry of rhymes with the poise and grit of a seasoned lyricist, making reference to a later popularized term by his blood cousin E-40 via the song and video "Captain Save A Hoe," released in July of 1994. But it's the title track that gives detail to Mac Dre's thoughts, emotions, and feelings about his unfortunate circumstances of being surveilled, harassed, and eventually thrown in jail:

"At first I thought I'd have to spank you, but Detective Nichelman, I'd like to thank you / You put me on the news and tried to spread that lie, then record sales jumped to an all-time high."

Wanda recalls the scrutiny her son's lyrics received during this trial, feeling as though the odds were stacked too high from the beginning for him to get adequate and fair treatment from the system. Vallejo's Lt. Richard Nichelman, whom Mac Dre addresses directly on the track, became more concerned with Dre's ability to make money than anything else.

In an interview with local Vallejo media the *Times Herald*, Nichelman said, "How do you allow a guy to do a record for profit when he's in custody?"

Kilo Curt recalls the genius of compiling the album from behind prison walls. "Khayree put the receiver right next to the speaker so Mac Dre could hear it and played the drum beat real low. Mac Dre would say, 'Man, I can't hear it,' Khayree said he needed to keep it low because 'It's on the same track with your vocal, so if I turn it up, it'll turn your vocal up. Just a little bit more Khayree, alright alright, that's good.' He's listening to the drum beat like that on that phone, and then the other phone is the phone with Khayree. He would have his voice going to the microphone, a CS1000 AKG, just to record his voice. So, one mic is Mac Dre and drums, one mic is Mac Dre only."

Kilo also remembers how sentimental and special the microphone Mac Dre used to record the album was. "Same mic Khayree recorded Tupac, Ray Luv, Mac Mall and others on," he said.

Of course, the logistics behind recording in jail were not easy from a sound quality perspective. Khayree recalled in an interview that "it was so noisy while he was in jail, you know. Motherfuckers yellin' and . . . I say, you ready? He said, 'yeah.' And I got a count on there, 'one and two.' But he couldn't hear because of the yelling, and he said, 'Hey, be cool muthafuckas, I'm tryna make a record!' and the jail would quiet down, and we'd go again."

Legendary Sacramento rapper, X-Raided, recalled in an interview running into Mac Dre while serving time in federal prison in the early 1990s and being impressed with his ability to record high-quality audio over the jail phone. Along with Mac Dre, he was one of the first rappers to have their lyrics used against them in court of law. X-Raided was arrested along with four other gang members in March 1992 for the murder of Patricia Harris, who investigators say was accidentally gunned down by a group of men in a botched attempt to shoot her two sons. He always maintained his innocence and was ultimately released twenty-six years after being found guilty, serving all but five years of his thirty-one year sentence.

X-Raided had been on his way to court at the Sacramento County Jail when he ran into Mac Dre in the holding pen. He explained that inmates fighting federal charges all over Northern County were transferred to Sacramento County for court. The first thing he noticed when walking into the cell was a giant afro protruding from the back of a crowd of people. As he made his way through the cell, he saw that it was none other than Mac Dre with his trademark afro sitting on the bench.

"We we're some of the only artists in the Bay Area actually being covered by the media. We were connected in that way," X-Raided said.

X-Raided says that Mac Dre taught him his method for recording raps through the jail phone. Up until this point, X-Raided had been recording verses to a voicemail, which would then get put onto a song.

"Dre told me to take the phone apart, right? And then we'd solder the mic cables to the transmitter, and then plug that into the mix board as the microphone," X-Raised said. "So now I call the phone and it goes straight into the mic board, then you call another phone, and they do the same, solder it and play the beat through that. So, I gotta listen to the beat on this one and spit the rhyme on that one."

Some of the local coverage of Mac Dre's incarceration came from KMEL radio, San Francisco's premier showcase of young DJs and on-air personalities like Sway Calloway and Chuy Gomez. KMEL dubbed themselves "The People's Station."

KMEL was doing its best to live up to its new slogan while broadcasting new urban-centric programming like *Street Soldiers*. While locked up and recording the album from Fresno County, Mac Dre spoke with radio talent at KMEL about his case. During the interview, Corey Dunn was exposed as the snitch who set him, Kilo Curt, and J. Diggs up. KMEL aired the interview, were visited by the FBI the following day, and were strongly encouraged not to play any portions of the interview containing their informant's name again. For a rap star on the rise who was barely twenty-one Mac Dre seemed to be a frequent point of emphasis for the FBI and its partners. While Billy Jams recalls visiting many locked-up rappers during that time in San Quentin and Santa Rita, he praises Mac Dre for his stance.

"Instead of being beaten down, he kept his head focused and fuckin' transcended it all and took it to the next level. It seemed like a setup to me when he was arrested after doing 'Punk Police.' At the time, we would sneak in recording material for 4-Tay when he was in the pen. It became a civil rights issue in the California penal system. You couldn't bring in a pencil or a piece of paper."

While Mac Dre sat in a Fresno prison awaiting trial, he called into KMEL Radio's very popular anti-gang program called *Street Soldiers*. In the interview, he ran down his version of the arrest and also made it known that the police had gotten a confidential informant to lie against him. The next day, KMEL Radio was once again visited by the FBI, who put the fear of God in the management and staff. Station officials were accused of trying to thwart the case and endanger the life of their key witness. In addition, the FBI informed the station management that Mac Dre's live interview was completely unauthorized. The result was no more live interviews from prison for Mac Dre, whose phone privileges were briefly revoked in prison.

Around this time, his partner and producer Khayree formed a Vallejo-based record label called Young Black Brotha, which was named after Mac Dre's first EP. He even recorded a new EP that featured Mac Dre's prison phone raps. The ultimate tribute came when Khayree released an LP from budding rapper Mac Mall. Khayree himself admits to being followed by the FBI after Mac Dre's arrest in Fresno. Perhaps his outspoken measures to get Dre released alarmed the authorities, but Khayree kept pushing. In an appearance on JuliTv, Khayree—with Young Black Brotha Records representatives in tow, including Ray Luv—delivered an impassioned speech about the ordeal Mac Dre was going through.

"Mac Dre is being conspired against for so many reasons," he says. "Young black brothas speaking out in the ghetto are always a target."

Mac Dre was sent to Lompoc Federal Penitentiary nearly five hours south of Vallejo. He was sentenced to five years, while Kilo and J. Diggs received ten. None of the men cooperated with authorities, choosing to stick to an honor system guided by the urban atmosphere they had become comrades within. Undoubtedly, the closeness that Kilo Curt and Mac Dre experienced on the streets of Vallejo intensified behind the walls of the federal penitentiary. Both men came to Lompoc on the same day, shackled together. As Kilo recalls, it all felt like "bullshit." That initial entry was rough for both men, but Mac Dre was lucky to already have money placed on his books. Dre looked out for Curt, providing food while his friend awaited some financial help from the outside. Kilo Curt, who had just turned nineteen, and Mac Dre, who was approaching twenty-two were newbies to federal prison life.

"On the bus, they got a dude named Black Bob from the Mexican mafia. They had twenty cars and helicopters following us. He was the biggest Sureño at the time. They were escorting him from court and brought him back to Lompoc."

Mac Dre and Kilo Curt were questioned about what they were in for and argued that there was no logical reason for them to be in federal prison with the likes of convicted murderers and cartel leaders.

"We kept telling each other, 'Cuddy, we aren't supposed to be here.' We even told the marshals, and they didn't give a fuck. They asked for our numbers and said, 'No, y'all supposed to be here.' We felt spooked. Not scared but concerned."

Kilo says he was originally sent to the K unit and Mac Dre was sent to the E unit. "Dre was in a dorm," Kilo says. "There were like 200 to 300 people in bunks. It was the most notorious one in the pen at the time. They would let us out the corridor to walk to our units. They close them when people come in. Every hour on the hour, the corridor would open for ten minutes. You could go to the yard, library, or wherever, but you only had ten minutes." Dre and Kilo exchanged some last words during the initial split in prison. "Cuddy, I hope I see you; I hope you make it, Cuddy."

Mac Dre and Kilo Curt faced further questioning from the inmates at Lompoc, who wanted to know why the two men were locked up. Kilo Curt remembers encountering prisoners from all over the country, since it was a federal penitentiary.

"New York cats would say, 'Where you from, shorty?' and the DC niggas said, 'Where you from, Joe?'" Kilo Curt says.

Eventually he was placed in a unit with a man named Shorty King from New York—a guy he describes as, "having that wavy hair with a part down the middle. A real old school New York motha-fucka." Kilo Curt was wary of the New York man's friendliness, having heard stories about becoming indebted to fellow prisoners by accepting gifts and favors without knowing. His new cellmate offered him shoes and some weed.

"I'm concerned this might be some okey-doke shit," Kilo Curt says. "I ain't finna be nobody bitch."

When the corridor opened that day and Kilo explained the situation and offer from Shorty King, Mac Dre was cautious with his young protégé: "Be cool, because it might be a setup."

"Nah nigga, we cool," Kilo Curt responded. "I even got a joint; let's go smoke."

Kilo Curt says it was only a few days later when both he and Mac Dre were called in for a second medical examination at the prison hospital. Prisoners at the time were spreading homophobic rumors and would joke that if you got a checkup at the prison hospital and received a call back within three days, you must have HIV or AIDS. Kilo Curt remembers feeling genuinely afraid when he got called back in.

"I'm stressing, like don't let me die like this. I saw Mac Dre coming on the day I was there, and he said, 'Cuddy, you see your name?' I said, 'Nigga your name is on there too!'"

Shortly before their time in the pen, NWA's Eazy-E had died from AIDS and NBA superstar Magic Johnson had retired from the NBA after contracting HIV. Prison doctors called Mac Dre into the back office first, leaving Kilo Curt to wait alone in the lobby. Dre emerged from the office minutes later with a wide smile on his face.

He said, "I don't know, just go in there. They said I'm good."

What Kilo would discover soon after going into the doctor's office was that he simply needed to take a urine test—a routine prison policy.

The first few weeks at Lompoc were eventful. Kilo Curt recalls early on a Hawaiian prisoner stabbing and killing two Mexican inmates. The prison was temporarily locked down for the next three weeks. To keep busy during the extended stint behind bars, Mac Dre, Kilo Curt, and J. Diggs lifted weights, played baseball, and constantly worked out. But they were also making sure to smoke good weed.

"We would work out for a month and then quit. We just looked for weed mostly. We smoked every day. We'd go maybe two or three days without smoking at the most. We smoked in our cells, the movie theater, outside. We burned tissue, rolled it real tight, and put deodorant against it, turning it into a makeshift incense to keep the smell under control."

Things began to feel more like home at Lompoc when six other Romper Room members were jailed there in 1993.

"We turned the units into the streets," Kilo Curt says. "Information was shared the same way. Every crew had their own section. We held our own crew in there with niggas from Baltimore, New Jersey, Los Angeles, white boys, Latin gangs."

The prison movie theater held 500 of the 1200 people housed at Lompoc. Most of the prison food was supplied by the Bush Brand and included tortillas, eggs, and beans every day. Canteen items like macaroni, cup-o-noodles, white chicken in a can, and tuna were staples. Card games were also a major fixture in Lompoc, especially one known as Dirty Hearts.

It was taught to Kilo Curt by his cellmate who told him, "In New York, they hit on top of the head when they lose real hard." It took Kilo Curt five straight losses and getting swatted on the head before he figured the game out.

Mac and Kilo each participated in the prison baseball league. Curt eventually took on the second base position for the team, called The Mandelas.

"Mac Dre tried out on the same day as me, and the first ball ate me up. So, I'm subconsciously fucked up," Kilo admits. "They like 'man, he ain't as good as he said he is.' Meanwhile, Mac Dre is playing left field, and he gotta run to chase down a fly, and he catches it over his shoulders. They like 'ooooh, this the one we should be taking!'"

Mac Dre made the Mandelas team on his first tryout with his Willie Mays-like catch. He took the opportunity to rub his quick success in Kilo Curt's face.

"You gotta hang in there, Cuddy!"

Kilo Curt responded to the chuckling Mac Dre, "Cuddy, don't try to act like you're better than me in baseball."

At the second tryout the following day, Kilo made the team. "Soon as we started having games, that nigga Mac Dre was horrible," Kilo Curt laughed. "He would get a ball hit to him while he was talking to people on the field and shit, not paying attention. We would yell 'DRE!' and he would run after it. The coach was like 'man, why you didn't make them catches like before during tryout?'"

Eventually, Mac Dre was turned into the "gofer" where he could play in the middle between the outfits—that way, he could run around and not disrupt the success of the team too much with his antics.

Football was no different for Mac Dre, according to Kilo. "Dre was catching everything Zulu the quarterback threw to him. He was looking like Jerry Rice out there! But when gametime came, he didn't catch shit."

The football team Kilo Curt and Mac Dre played on in Lompoc was called Up North and consisted of pimps and players with rollers in their hairs, Kilo Curt remembers.

He admits the Up North football team couldn't afford to be overly competitive and could only really beat "Indian and white teams." Eventually, teams got split up, and the Los Angeles Bloods team wanted the leftovers from the Up North roster. Once the two teamed up, they became "B& B (Bloods and the Bay)." Before acquiring the struggling Up North team, the Bloods' very successful outfit hadn't been scored on in more than seven years. That streak ended when the quarterback threw a Hail Mary, which was caught by Mac Dre.

"He went for forty yards, then hit the icky shuffle and the centipede and we carried him off the field," Kilo laughs, remembering that day. "We didn't even win the game, but it was the first score. He was always a character. The Mac Dre character was real. Then they started calling him Silky Slim."

Mac Dre's character blossomed behind bars. He gained a new confidence by simply being the funny, charming man his mother and The Crest friends had already known him to be. Mac Dre's one-liners caused a frenzy in Lompoc, which inspired other inmates to nearly lose it, professing their love for "Silky Slim." Mac Dre's style, charm, and even walk were topics of discussion behind prison walls. Kilo chuckles thinking back on his goofy walk around the prison yard.

"He had this walk. It was tall and upright, and he looked kinda like Popeye when he hit the spinach and both his arms started moving toward you. But he was hella skinny, and it was his body that would go up instead of the arms. You could tell it was Dre walking toward you from a mile away."

Kilo continued, "And his eyes were big and bubbly like Mr. Furley from *Three's Company*. He had a smirk even when he had bad news. Like he enjoyed telling you some shit. I'd have to tell the nigga to give me a drink first."

Mac Dre, Kilo Curt, and J. Diggs made sure to keep their ears to the streets and always kept abreast of developments in the independent and mainstream music scene. In 1993, Mac Mall, who was working with Khayree, released his first album, *Illegal Business*. His video for "Ghetto Theme" was directed by Tupac Shakur and walked viewers through a tale of respect, deceit, and karma, told from the eyes of a young black man from the ghetto.

Mac Mall released his follow-up to *Illegal Business* in April 1996, titled *Untouchable*. It came out under a new music imprint out of New York City called Relativity Records. The album peaked at number thirty-five on the billboard chart and birthed two powerful anthems, "Get Right" and "Let's Get a Telly." Mac Dre would remember constantly seeing the familiar face of Tupac Shakur in the visiting room at Lompoc. Tupac's stepfather, Mutulu Shakur—who was also there for conspiring to rob a bank—looked out for Mac Dre and crew as often as he could. Kilo Curt recalls the many conversations he had with Mutulu and other older inmates who looked out for the three of them.

"So many lifers and murderers knew we didn't belong there," Kilo Curt says. "We were young kids and ruthless. They became uncles and big brothers to us. We learned the ropes. We were learning how to use resources. Muslims, Italians, Aryan brotherhood, dirty white boys, Mexican mafia, Norteños. Us being from Cali, we never saw people from different states in one place until we got to prison. We learned the difference between boroughs."

Mutulu once told the youngsters from Vallejo, "Y'all going down a crazy path. Y'all betta learn something and take it to the streets. Stop being knuckleheads."

The insight was something he likely shared with Tupac, who began to battle his own enemies in the streets and in courtrooms across the country.

Mac Dre, unsurprisingly, found ways to perfect his craft as a musician while locked away in Lompoc. He was able to perform behind bars at different prison events and would even rap with fellow inmates during recreation time. Even the correctional officers became fans, according to Wanda. She said even prison couldn't break the carefree spirit of Mac Dre, who learned while inside never to take life for granted. Through all the brutality that's seen and experienced in American prisons, Mac Dre never lost his hope for a better future. He never stopped trying to figure out ways to get himself and his loved ones out of their precarious situations in Black America.

Mac Dre lost another friend while locked away in Lompoc in 1995. His close friend and DJ, Cee, died on August 29th in a drive-by shooting in Vallejo. Mac Dre was often reaching out to and receiving correspondence from local media outlets like *Strivin'* magazine, owned by Doxx. One lengthy letter to Doxx details Dre's feelings about his time in jail:

> "What's hatnin' folks? I'm gettin' at you to return some of that Bay love you've shown a young playa caught up in the Feds. I'm sorry it took so long to respond, but I was trying to return to the town unannounced, and I didn't want to spoil thangz, ya know? But after receiving your constant correspondence and newsletters, I recognized your realness.
>
> I'm glad to see another real muthafucka represent that Bay thang wholeheartedly!! Me and my folks from the Romper Room crew are representin' to the fullest, lettin' fools in this federal system know that the Bay Area ain't no joke!! It's mutha-fuckas from Mare Island to the Virgin Islands in the Feds, and they know that the Bay consists of pimps, playas, gangstas, and big bankta! I'm up here lacin' these fools with that shit that you've been missin'.
>
> That uncut, super sucka free Romper Room game that only Mac Dre can serve! You think muthafuckas are out there pop-pin' now, huh, wait till they get a load of me!! I'm nothin' cor-rectable and ain't to be fucked with, and you can best believe I'm comin' home to reclaim my throne folks (and you can print that)! I'm about to sign with . . . Well, let's just say the mutha-fucka with the biggest bank!! I gots to come home to somethin' extremely phat so I can clown those smirks who did the wrong thing during my bid."

Mac Dre climbed out from the dark meadows of Lompoc Federal Penitentiary as a free man on August 2nd, 1996 after a total of four years and four months behind bars. He was ready to turn a new leaf. This would be the beginning of a new phase in Mac Dre's career, as his music slowly became more focused on having fun and partying versus the inequalities of The Crest and violence—though there's still plenty of that in his later music as well, because you can take Mac Dre out of The Crest, but you can't take The Crest out of Mac Dre.

IN HIS OWN WORDS: GETTING OUT OF PRISON

This interview originally appeared in Issue Two of *Strivin'* magazine (1997).

Let everyone know what's up with Mac Dre now?

What's up? This is young Mac Dre, fresh out the Feds, handlin' business. This is my second week out. I'm already startin' my own record label, Romp Records. We puttin' together like a sixteen-song compilation that will be out on December 10th. It's called Mac Dre Presents The Rompalation with the 187 Fac, Mac Mall, Da 5 Footaz, JT The Bigga Figga, Dangerous Dame, Jay Tee from N2Deep, Beesh, San Quinn, Seff Da Gaffla, Messy Marv, Dubee aka Sugawolf Pimp, Coolio Da Unda Dogg, Young Lay, me, and various artists that's gonna be on my label like Stevie D (PSD), Doscha, and Young Web. So, I'm just in here workin' immediately, tryin' to get back out in the mix.

I heard you're also workin' on a solo album to come after that.

In early '97, I'm gonna drop a solo album on Romp Records, and that's just gonna be the bomb. Both of 'em gonna be the bomb, but this is just a taste to let you know what you're in store for. The first one is just like an icebreaker. I'm just lettin' people know that I'm back and the things that's on my mind and where I'm gonna take my corner of the rap game to.

Are you talkin' at all about the case that sent you to the Feds?

I'm not gonna talk too much about the case because one thing I found out while bein' locked up is that when you fuckin' with the

Feds, it's a no-win situation. I can do all the rappin' and talkin' about mothafuckas I want, and the end result is I'll be back behind bars hopin' to be out again. I'ma concentrate on makin' money and doin' what I gotta do to keep my pockets extra fat.

You were down for four and a half years, right?

Four years, four months.

Most of your time you spent writin'? That's what you told me last time.

I did a lot of writin' and a lot of game soakin'. A lot of watchin' and a lot of listenin'.

Who's workin' on the compilation as far as production?

We got K-Lou, Khayree, Ferg, Johnny Z. We tryin' to get (Mike) Mosley to do some thangs and that's about it.

Now that you're out, are you doing things a little different as far as your own personal behavior?

Well, I'm doin' things a lot different, because before I went to jail, I was like in the hood 24-7, didn't wanna leave the hood, and was just a straight hood person—a straight hood nigga. Now I'm concentratin' more on handlin' my business as far as the rap thang and stayin' shaded and out people's way.

So, you saw what you were doin' before is not the thing to do anymore?

I wasn't doin' nothin' wrong really, but just hangin' out. Everybody hang out, but you get caught up hangin' out. And then when you on celebrity status. . . . See, I wasn't thinkin' about me bein' on celebrity status. I was just thinkin', "Man, I'm just a regular nigga. I just rap. I can be out here just like everybody else." But now I see when you on celebrity status the attitude that people have towards you change differently. You just can't be out like every other ordinary dude.

So, you saw that the more you came up, the more other people were tryin' to bring you down?

It's a lot of jealous, envious people out there that hate to see the next person doin' good. I was lookin' at it like I'm not gonna change because I'm from here and this is what I do. I'm not thinkin' I'm better than nobody. This is just what I do, and what I do has got me successful, but some people can't take it for that. And I'm not just talkin' about dudes from the neighborhood. I'm talkin' about police, city hall representatives, people in the music industry.

Now while you were gone, a lot of bad things happened as far as people with your label: DJ Cee got killed, Young Lay got shot, and then what happened with his baby and girlfriend. How did that affect you while you were in there when you heard about it?

Well, it hurt me. Especially DJ Cee, 'cause he was with me from day one, and I hate to hear what happened to Young Lay too 'cause that's my folks. I watched him grow up and all that hurted me. But the end result was it motivated me to take this thing to the next level—to a higher level—and be successful for my folks that's not here right now like DJ Cee and The Mac.

He (DJ Cee) was one of the original DJs from Vallejo, right?

Yeah.

Was he the one who got you started?

Naw, The Mac got me started rappin'.

How did he influence you when you first started off rappin'?

I was in the boy's ranch. I got released from the boy's ranch, and when I came out, he had a maxi-single out and I was like, "Man, you makin' records? I'ma try to start rappin'." So, I started rappin', makin' demos. Studio Ton had a little four-track studio downtown, and I was fuckin' with him, and when my partner The Mac heard my shit, he took it to Khayree. And when Khayree heard it, he said, "We got to have him on wax."

Last time I interviewed you, we talked about how things were before between the Crestside, Southside, Hillside, and all that. Now that you're out, have you associated with any of those people that you used to have beef with?

I talked to a few of 'em. The only one I haven't talked to; I think is forty. He probably on celeb status somewhere chillin'. But now it's no animosity. The only conflict I got is with my bankroll. I'm tryin' to have my bank as fat as possible.

So, your label, Romp Records—who are you gonna put out on that?

Romp Records, I'm the president. My partner right there is D-Con, that's my executive. A female by the name of Pam, she runnin' A&R,

and my cousin Los is doin' promotion. We got artists from here to New York, Compton, but we gonna start at home in the Crestside.

Who's gonna be first?

Remember Coolio that rapped on "California Livin'" with me? That's my first artist. He changed his name to Da Unda Dogg. After that, we got two artists that's comin' out at the same time: Doscha and Stevie D (PSD).

Can you talk about a few of the things that are gonna be on your first album?

I might come with some stuff I wrote while I was in the pen, but I'm thinkin' about just lockin' up with a Khayree DAT and just writin' all new shit.

What's some of the stuff you're talkin' about?

It's just like I'm a good storyteller. I got a lot of story raps, and I could take you to the hood and put you on an all-night money mission, grindin' from eight o'clock at night to four o'clock in the mornin'. I got raps about that. I got raps about takin' you to a party where suckas is playa hatin' on you and you have to handle your business. I take you in different atmospheres, and then I let people know that the end result of doin' the things that I did is the penitentiary. That's cool if you choose to do it, but just remember the consequences. You gonna be in the pen or, like my homeboy The Mac, be in the casket.

Since you left and now, you're back and you've had a few weeks to circulate and talk to people, how do you see people's attitudes?

Since I been back, I've seen nothin' but love. From people from my neighborhood to Bay Area artists, everywhere I go they greet me with open arms. Everybody thinks I'm gonna be real successful, so I can't let nobody down.

Do you see how times have changed a little bit?

Times have changed and people have changed, because when I left, it was more of a bond between Bay Area artists. Now you got these people over here, you got people that moved up out of the Bay that don't mess with the people they used to mess with, and that kinda tripped me out.

How else have you seen the Bay Area rap scene change as far as more artists and different areas comin' up?

Yeah, everybody rappin' now. When I left, people was just buyin' tapes. Now everybody makin' tapes.

Do you see that as good?

Naw, I don't see that as good because some of that stuff be bullshit, and it be cloudin' up the industry. If somebody go to a record store and they got a hundred tapes up there, you might overlook somethin' that's good because you might see somethin' that has a good album cover on it and think that's the bomb—and you really lookin' over the bomb. I think people who don't know how to rap should try somethin' else. And if you friends with somebody that's tryin' to rap and they don't know how to rap, tell 'em man, "You don't know how to rap! Give it up!"

I heard you had a little BBQ party, a surprise thing that happened (upon your release).

Yeah, they threw me a little surprise party. Warren G came up, Dru Down, the Luniz. It was cool.

Did you know them before?

Nope. They came just to show. They remember me from back in the day.

In the interview, Mac Dre says he spent his time in prison wisely, watching and learning from the older and wiser inmates. He said he had a change of heart since getting locked up.

"I'm concentrating more on handling business as far as the rap thing goes.

CHAPTER EIGHT
THE ROMPALATION BEGINS

"I was twenty-one when I went to Lompoc. You know how you hear stories about the pen when you're young, like people getting stabbed up? I wasn't scared, but I didn't know what to expect. I was prepared for the worst. So, when I got up in there, you wouldn't think so many people from the Bay Area would be there. People from Oakland and Richmond, so people knew about me. I was the representative for the Bay Area in the federal penitentiary, you feel me? I'm the poster child. So every so often, I'd have to go in the band room and eat a rapper from wherever, New York, L.A., wherever they came from! People brought 'em up there in the band room to see if they could get down with Mac Dre. It gave me a little bit of respect when I was there. I was up there as a Mob Figga with the Mob Figaz cause I could entertain them."

—Mac Dre

*T*he *Rompalation* album Mac Dre referenced in his interview with *Strivin'* magazine released on December 10th, 1996, just four months after his release from Lompoc FCI. *The Rompalation's* premiere track was headlined by Mac Dre himself, where his usual game was soaked and passed onto hungry listeners. With the Looie Crew-assisted track, "Uninvited," Mac Dre and friends created a classic posse cut full of street tales about car rides, getting drunk, and leaving no witnesses.

The Rompalation turned out to be one of Mac Dre's most trend-setting projects in his early career. The use of the music mashup or compilation can be seen as a prequel to mixtapes in the early 2000s, which were widely popular on the streets of New York. The collaboration concept from an album viewpoint was new and refreshing and allowed artists from different parts of the Bay Area and the state of California to extend and expand their fan bases. Other power-house compilations of the time include *West Coast Bad Boyz,* which was executive produced by Master P. *The Rompalation* featured San Francisco recording artists Seff Tha Gaffla, JT The Bigga Figga and Messy Marv (credited as MessCalen), and Vallejo artists Baby Bash, Jay Tee, E.B. Daddy of Da Hood, Mac Mall, and Coolio Da Unda Dogg. On the cross-state track "LA 2 Da Bay," Da 5 Footaz from Southern California showed off as a female outfit that would soon sign to Def Jam.

After his stint in Lompoc, Mac Dre was intent on increasing his output of music through doing whatever albums, compilations, and features he could find. Just months after *The Rompalation* hit stores, Khayree presented his own compilation project *The Blackalation— The World Is Yours* on July 18th, 1997. Mac Dre officially appeared on three of the sixteen tracks from super-producer Khayree. *The Blackalation* album was released under Young Black Brotha Records, a title Khayree used with the blessing of Mac Dre, who coined the term years prior on his EP of the same name. On track eleven, Khayree leans into a slightly adjusted sample from Oakland megastars Tony! Toni! Toné!'s "It Never Rains (In Southern California)," for which Mac Dre delivers arguably some of the smoothest, most effortless, and most memorable verses of his career.

Mac Dre's cool, easygoing delivery makes "Rainin' Game" a top play in his expansive catalog. In his third bar on verse one, Dre shows love to longtime friend Dubee, who was the first artist to feature Mac Dre on a record when he was released from prison in 1996. On the solo project from Dubee, who was a month shy of turning twenty-two for his debut *Dubee aka Sugawolf*, the Young Black Brotha signee leaves an entire song open for his mentor Mac Dre to roam free. In the appropriately titled "Mac Dre (Game I'm Spittin')," Dre kicks his usual pimp and Mac lines with finesse and shows great appreciation for Dubee in the outro of the cut: "Young Dubee, you big ol' pimp you, love you folks." Mac Dre and Dubee would grow to share a special bond, becoming fast friends and frequent collaborators in a music business filled with snakes and bad-faith executives.

Mac Dre did a good job focusing on music and making up for lost time in the months and years after he was released, but it wasn't all perfect. He violated the terms of his parole by smoking weed at the end of 1997 after sixteen months of freedom. He ended up going back to prison for just under two years, getting out for the final time in 1999.

"In the *High Times* magazine, in the very back, there was an advertisement he saw about Backwoods, and somehow he thought he was free to smoke, that weed wouldn't show up in his system if he smoked it in a Backwoods," Kilo Curt said.

Less than two weeks after Kilo spoke with Mac Dre about the *High Times* ad, he received a call: "Cuddy, I got hit with fourteen dirties (positive drug tests)—I'm on the run!"

Mac Dre was quickly apprehended and sent back to prison. He returned home for good in 1999, three months before Kilo Curt was finally released from Lompoc for the Fresno bank case.

Kilo and J. Diggs spent the better part of ten years in federal prison. Doing that much time can change a man, and it's not always easy transitioning back into society. There's an underlying fear and paranoia surrounding leaving a place you've been for a decade—a place that regiments your meals and activity time. The blast of stimuli after reentering society can be too much for some. Kilo remembers having a hard time feeling free in those early days. He thought he was about to get rearrested at any moment, even though he hadn't committed any new crimes. He said he read a news report about an unnamed member of the Romper Room Gang being arrested, and he became fixated on the idea that it was him and that the news story had accidentally gotten released early.

"I was thinking it was me when I got out," he says.

Kilo continued to feel wary as he transitioned from FCI Lompoc to FCI Englewood in Colorado, where he finished out his prison bid. He gave his mother detailed instructions on how he wanted to leave

FCI Englewood, telling her to rent him a limousine that would have a brand-new Oakland Raiders sweatsuit waiting for him in the back.

"I came out the prison gate that day, and the first thing I saw was a black town car," Kilo says. "I was pissed! I'm thinking 'what the fuck is going on? Is this the feds?'"

The driver of the black town car confirmed Kilo's name, and he reluctantly shuffled into the vehicle as he was told again and again that he was being taken to the airport. In the back of the limo, Kilo called his mother to complain about the transportation, admitting he was spooked about the whole ordeal. His mother informed him that his ticket was ready at the airport and not to worry. However, his guard remained high as the driver coasted past the federal building and numerous downtown skyscrapers. His anxiety over getting arrested only worsened on the flight between Denver and Seattle.

"I'm getting arrested in Seattle is all I'm thinking," Kilo recalls. "They were playing mental games! Finally, I got to Oakland."

Kilo remembers seeing Mac Dre walking down Simelton Street on his first day out, surprised to see his friend maneuvering with no car.

"I'm like 'what the fuck, he's walking?'" Kilo says. "Then we hugged, we got emotional."

Mac Dre told Kilo that he didn't have any money and that it was "stupid out here."

The two walked through the old neighborhood as Mac Dre announced to anyone who would listen, "Kilo back! Kilo back!"

He was beginning to feel like he was finally home. The fear and paranoia slowly began to dissipate in those early days. The first day he was out of prison, Kilo says, he popped ecstasy pills. Five days later, when he received a call from Mac Dre asking about his pill consumption, he fessed up.

"Mac Dre straight up said, 'You on pills?' I said, 'Yeah!'"

Mac Dre hung up the phone, and less than fifteen minutes later, he was at Kilo's house. "Cuddy," he started. "I didn't wanna get you on pills, but since you're on 'em, let's go!"

With no car and very little money, Kilo and Dre began to plot how the latter could reclaim his throne as the premier Bay Area rap stylist. It was the summer of 1999, and Mac Dre vowed to learn the mechanics of the local music business. He already had a name that rang bells throughout the streets of Oakland, Vallejo, San Francisco, and beyond. He encouraged Kilo to begin investing his time in learning the music industry.

"He would say, 'Cuddy, if you wanna be my business partner, you gotta learn more shit,'" Kilo says. "You can get Cuddy money, or you can get partner money. When he'd get mad, he'd say, 'Dame Dash wouldn't do that, Cuddy wouldn't do that.' That's how I became his business partner. He was doing a lot of multitasking, and I started to get serious and really learn the ins and outs."

Kilo was a fast learner, and he had an elevated taste in modern-day rap music that expanded beyond the Bay Area. He first wanted to see if he could get Mac Dre signed, or even a distribution deal, from one of the bigger labels in order to gauge interest. He reached out to Cash Money Records in 2000.

"I figured maybe we need to sign with them. I called, and they were ready to put me on the phone with any of the top niggas," Kilo says.

But ultimately, a deal never worked out. While the opportunity of signing to a major record label would have helped Mac Dre's status and visibility in the mainstream, the likelihood that his finances would be threatened by the signing was very real. Many independent recording artists around the Bay Area, including RBL Posse and JT The Bigga Figga, were selling records in the hundreds of thousands and doing so without the powerful hand of major record labels and distributors, thus holding onto a larger share of the profits. The balancing process turned Kilo into a true and efficient businessman for his longtime friend.

The conditions of Mac Dre's parole were abundantly clear: he was not to return to Vallejo, California or associate with known criminals. This all but permanently cut him off from The Crest. He decided instead to relocate to Sacramento, which would eventually be dubbed "Macramento" due to Mac Dre's infamous presence and his consistent steady schedule of recording and performing. Romp Records also began to host and throw their own events in those early Sacramento days.

"We started getting into raves and shit," Kilo says. "That's how we started Thizz. I threw a party one time and called it the 'Thizz Party.' One party we threw was with Mac Dre and Lil Bruce in Fairfield. They shut it down thinkin' Bruce and Mac Dre were at war. But Mac Dre and Bruce became cool, which was crazy, because

Bruce had shot at me before. I thought it was impossible for them to be cool."

Kilo remembers Mac Dre telling him after he was out of prison that they needed to squash any prior conflicts in order to move on from their past. Mac Dre wasn't trying to lean into past disputes, instead choosing to take his music career on a more positive, hedonistic path. But old habits sometimes die hard, and it wasn't long before Mac Dre found himself feuding with an old Vallejo associate and collaborator.

Mac Dre's first proper album since coming home, *Rapper Gone Bad*, came out on September 28, 1998. It included a song called "Mac Stabber" that directly addresses issues Mac Dre had with Mac Mall and his former producer Khayree. Mac Dre felt that Khayree and Mac Mall weren't showing him the type of love he deserved upon his second release from prison. This was a particularly hard time for Mac Dre, as he didn't even have a car and wasn't allowed back in his former neighborhood where most of his connections were.

Mac Mall hadn't had an album out since the year Mac Dre returned home, but that didn't necessarily hurt his image. His 1993 classic *Illegal Business?* captured the attention of longtime fans and label heads across the nation. His frequent collaborations with Tupac, who was murdered weeks after Mac Dre's release, made him arguably the hottest rap artist in Vallejo during the period of Mac Dre's incarceration. In 1996, Mall had appeared on the compilation CD *America Is Dying Slowly* alongside Wu-Tang Clan, Fat Joe, Common, and 8Ball and MJG. In 1999, he started his own label, Sessed Out Records. The first release was the compilation *Mac Mall Presents the*

Mallennium. Mac Mall also released the sequel to his major label debut, *Illegal Business? 2000,* which birthed one of his greatest songs: "Wide Open."

Illegal Business? 2000 reached 185 on the US Billboard 200, while reaching fifty-four and seven on the US Top R&B/Hip Hop Albums (Billboard) and US Heatseekers Albums (Billboard), respectively.

One of Mac Mall's frequent collaborators at the time was San Francisco music executive and producer JT The Bigga Figga. Back in 1993, JT and Mac Mall joined forces to drop one of the most well-recognized Bay Area rap songs of all time with "Game Recognize Game." On Mac Dre's *Stoopid Doo Doo Dumb* in 1998, JT The Bigga Figga introduced the album with a high-energy verbal walkthrough.

In 1999, Mac Mall and JT completed production on their independent film, *Beware of Those,* with a subsequent soundtrack months later. One of the standout tracks from the soundtrack, "What's the Decision," featured Vallejo's new top gun in rap, E-40. While Mac Mall and Mac Dre were not seeing eye to eye, it appeared their missions were the same: get Vallejo on the national stage.

"Mac Stabber," a simultaneously brilliant and bitter moment on "Rapper Gone Bad," sees Mac Dre attacking Mac Mall with surprising vengeance, catching another prison flashback: "That nigga left me for dead when I was doin' time in jail / Couldn't shoot a nigga naythin' when he was havin' major mail."

The catalyst of the short-lived beef between the two is not entirely clear, but it is certain that Mac Mall genuinely felt nothing but love and honor for Mac Dre. In an interview promoting *Illegal*

Business? 2000 with Bay Area journalist JR Valrey, Mac Mall discussed his early start in the business.

"Man, the Mac . . . I'm kids of them, though, you feel? When I came out, if you remember, that's when Mac Dre went to jail, The Mac had gotten killed, and it was now on me to represent Crestside music, Cutthroat music, what we do. If I didn't come out at that time, we would have been silent," Mac Mall says. "I was blessed to hook up with Khayree, you feel? And me and him put together what some call a classic."

Clearly, Mac Mall not only perceived some level of debt to the "Macs" that he came up under musically, but he felt a sense of pride and responsibility to hold up The Crest and Vallejo in everything he did.

However, what prison did the second time around for Mac Dre's musical career was open his eyes to something else—a larger world outside of Vallejo, California and the Bay Area. It was a beautiful time for Mac Dre personally and creatively, as he began to burrow into the sound that would begin to make him more famous than he'd ever been before.

Rapper Gone Bad showed a matured and rejuvenated Mac Dre revisiting familiar topics with a newfound perspective that left his music feeling fresh and alive. The song "I'm a Thug" features PSD and longtime partner Dubee, while "Valley Joe" unites rival turfs Hillside (B-Legit, Lil' Bruce) and Crestside (Mac Dre, PSD). The album features some of Mac Dre's most iconic songs, including the prison meditation "I've Been Down" and the regional hit "Fire." The album makes for perhaps the best introduction to Mac Dre for novice fans because it showcases his knack for mixing humor, wisdom, and real storytelling to take listeners through the streets of Vallejo.

Producers Lev Berlak & Will 'Flexxx' Hankins cover a wide spectrum with the minimal funk of the title track (with added old-school flavor courtesy of Malcolm McLaren and The World's Famous Supreme Team) alongside the melodic "Fish Head Stew," the stutter-stepping "Fortytwo Fake," the trunk-rattling "Fuck Off The Party," and the aforementioned "Mac Stabber." In both verses of "Fire," sandwiched around hook help from Harm and a verse from East Dallas native Big Lurch, Mac Dre uses his trademark in and out, stop and go cadence while riding the beat with a subtle intensity.

Mac Dre would go on to drop four solo projects in the next three years, all while building a solid pipeline for artists he worked with to get distribution deals through City Halls Records. He was also able to tour extensively through Northern California, Oregon, Fresno, and Kansas City, whose regional hip-hop scene shared a close relationship with the Bay Area. A few weeks before his thirty-first birthday, Mac Dre released the first of two albums that year, appropriately titled *Mac Dre's the Name*, which dropped on June 13th, 2001. Dre continued his cross-state relationships on "Dangerous," which featured Southern California rap bosses Bad Azz and Daz Dillinger. The only other feature on the album came on the track "I Gotta Go" with female Sacramento rapper Marvaless, a protégée of C-Bo.

Just six months later, he released *It's Not What You Say . . . It's How You Say It* on November 20th, 2001, as his sixth studio project (not including compilations and features). The album is flooded with features, including Oakland's Richie Rich and Keak Da Sneak,

San Francisco's Messy Marv, and DJ Quik collaborator Suga Free. Usual suspects from Vallejo like Dubee, PSD, and J. Diggs also make appearances. While neither of the 2001 albums produced monster hits like "California Livin'" or "Too Hard for the Fuckin' Radio," Mac Dre's high volume of new music and soon-to-be-legendary work ethic made sure that his name stayed in the mix and laid a foundation for what a Thizz Entertainment record is supposed to sound like.

Mac Dre began setting up studios across the Bay Area. He had spots in Oakland and Sacramento that each helped establish himself and his extended crew as shrewd businessmen, label owners, and—in the case of Thizzelle Washington himself—an actual budding music star in his own right. The studios helped make the Bay Area a more desirable and profitable place for the music industry and helped to lay roots that still exist today. The studio in Sacramento, stationed on more than an acre of land, boasted several exterior buildings in the back and a large pool. It was typically referred to as The Compound. The Compound would also come to be known as "Rappers Island," because the cell service was so bad it felt like you were stranded in the middle of the ocean, with nothing to do but rap to kill time. Mac Dre created a "work only" atmosphere that helped contribute to his crew's prolific output during these years.

"Nobody was being charged to record," Kilo says. "We paid for everything in the studio. We also had a studio off Poplar in West Oakland called Soundwave. All the rappers knew you could lose your spot on a song if it wasn't dope. As soon as the 'owner of the building' came in, it was on. They'd be like, 'Hopefully, I make the cut on this song, Cuddy,'" Kilo remembers, laughing.

Kilo continues: "At one point, Keak Da Sneak was living in Sacramento with Mac Dre. At Rappers Island, we did Cutthroat Committee, Lil Bruce, Rydah J. Klyde projects. Mac Dre had a vision of what he wanted to do. He was offered a deal before he died, and Mac Dre wanted to sign The Luniz, Messy Marv, San Quinn, Keak, The Mob Figaz, and Cutthroat Committee. He said, 'Instead of me signing, just let me sign all the hot niggas.'"

Kilo says Mac Dre wanted to be entirely independent and self-made. He didn't want greedy record labels capitalizing off their artwork anymore. He knew it would be an uphill battle, but he was determined to stay independent as much as possible for the sake of his crew and the longevity of the music.

Mac Dre soon met a young man who would help sharpen up his stage presence and craft one of the hallmark creations of the rap icon's legacy. Before "Thizz Dance" became a phenomenon for Mac Dre in 2002, Brian, a Vallejo native who worked at the Circuit City in Concord, California, was just nineteen years old and selling computers, car stereos, and the like. B-Luv, the name that he performed under, was a prototypical hustler born and bred in Vallejo's Crestside neighborhood, using any and all natural resources he could muster to turn a profit.

His video production company was one of his major side hustles, as he allowed Circuit City's computer department to pay the bills. One day while at work, B-Luv met a customer who approached him asking for a job. He told the customer—a white kid named Justin Lomax—to put his name down as a reference so he could secure credit if he was hired, even though they didn't really know one another.

Soon after, Justin was hired, and Brian received his credit for knowing how to hustle. The two bonded instantly, becoming friends with a shared interest in entertainment and video production.

"I showed him some stuff . . . one of which was the sideshow documentary I was working on (*Exhibition of Speed*). He showed me what he was doing, mostly skateboard videos," B-Luv says.

During the East Bay extravaganza known as Black Saturday (a party, sideshow, and networking playground), B-Luv met the man he describes as his favorite rapper.

"When I was nineteen, I went to Black Saturday a lot!" he says. "They also used to have the UC Davis frat parties, and I was known for stepping through and giggin' and shit."

At one fateful frat party attended by none other than Mac Dre and Dubee, the rappers witnessed a crowd frenzy around a dancing B-Luv.

"Niggas was in here goin' crazy," B-Luv remembers. "Mac Dre came up to me and was like, 'Man, you were out there getting' it.' He showed love. Dubee was like, 'Oh yeah, that's the little Cuddy from the hood.'"

At the time, Mac Dre was already known for an entertaining stage show and often worked with Sacramento's Sumthin' Terrible to get the newest dance moves across.

"He told me one day, 'Man, Cuddy, the way you be giggin', can't nobody fuck with you," B-Luv says. Dre took the way B-Luv danced and the way he danced and created the Thizz Dance, named after a slang term for ecstasy and defined by its loud and rambunctious style. "When you look at the video for 'Thizzle Dance' and he says 'wipe the sweat off me face'—that's me! I'm in the video!"

Black Saturdays were a highly influential weekly get-together, a mashup of dance crews and rappers, producers and the average citizen, and folks from various communities looking to network and hook up. Major Bay Area turfs were represented far and wide during Black Saturday episodes, from Richmond and Oakland to San Francisco and Vallejo.

"It was just an organic thing. A Bay Area thing," B-Luv adds.

There was a certain creative spirit in the air during these times. Everyone was in the prime of their music-making abilities. There were few to no conflicts with other crews in the streets, and people were enjoying the overall party vibes of the whole era. Everything Mac Dre did seemed to be notable, from his clothes to the way he talked in interviews. This was a man who could create a lingo that was only his—and that was almost indecipherable to the common man's ear. This was someone who could single-handedly bring back Hawaiian T-shirts and make them cool again. Others surrounding Mac Dre knew they were sitting on a goldmine. B-Luv and Justin Lomax decided to team up with Mac Dre for a new documentary series where they would just follow him around. The idea seemed novel back in 2001, but nowadays, this is standard operating for any artist looking to break out. Mac Dre was a reality television star before it was cool to be one. He was an artist perennially ahead of his time. If he would have lived to see the social media era, he could have been as big as Snoop Dogg.

The documentary series, titled *TREALTV*, was the brainchild of Mac Dre but with help and heavy influence from B-Luv. Before production began, B-Luv noticed that Mac Dre spent a lot of time just filming himself—in cars, talking, rapping, and running errands.

"I was like, 'Nah Cuddy, nah, you're too big to be recording yourself.' So, me and Mac Dre sat down and talked it out."

Much of that footage ended up being used for the hilarious, groundbreaking TREALTV documentary.

The TREALTV documentary was an immediate hood classic. It was a mix of hood clips and videos of Mac Dre performing and just hanging out. They became so popular that it even introduced Mac Dre's name into circles he hadn't reached before. Oakland freestyle king Mistah Fab first heard of the Hyphy Hero through TREALTV documentaries in the early 2000s. For TREALTV—the name of which is a playful spin on Ahmad Rashad's *Real TV*—they needed to be constantly filming and producing.

"Man, we filmed everything no matter what," B-Luv recalls. "Going to the liquor store? Turn the camera on. I just knew how important it was to document our lives, of course not knowing what was going to happen to the Cuddy eventually. But now that footage is even more important. And it's rare. It was all about having fun, getting shit captured. It was easy working with Mac Dre."

While Justin Lomax built the entire set for *TREALTV* in a rented studio in the North Bay, where Mac Dre positioned himself in much of the film, other shooting locations included the state of Hawaii and the city of Las Vegas. In Sin City, Kilo Curt recalls a fist fight that he believes gave birth to the use of popular 2000s eyewear termed "stunna shades."

"I'm on federal parole, not even supposed to be in Vegas, right? I got hit in the arm at the start of the fight, but I was on that Thizz, so at first, I wasn't feeling shit," Kilo says. "Then I got hit in the leg; I'm down to one knee when I feel a six-foot-eight nigga jump on my back!"

When he saw a man pull out handcuffs, he knew the men they were fighting with were undercover police officers.

"I wouldn't let them handcuff me," he adds. "I see Mac Dre and I'm like, 'Don't let them handcuff me.' The nigga turned his back on me. I yelled, 'I'm the victim!' They finally took the handcuffs off and threw us out of the venue we were in."

Kilo, whose eyes were bruised up from the fight, confesses that Mac Dre was unscathed. He later retold events of the night to everyone who wasn't there personally, including rapper Yukmouth.

"Mac Dre kept saying, 'Let them see yo eyes, Kilo. Look what they did to his ass.' This is when stunna shades came out," Kilo adds.

On the Hawaii leg of their *TREALTV* production, two cameras were in constant rotation as they walked up and down the strip in Waikiki. Mac Dre was carefree during the trip, happy to be away from home and with friends who he considered family.

"He paid for everybody to go out there," B-Luv says. "That's crazy for not having a deal. We were about forty deep. Mac Dre brought people together, even the artists."

In Hawaii, the group performed at various venues, visited the local radio station, and, as B-Luv says, "brought the Bay Area energy with us."

A noteworthy scene from *TREALTV* came when Mac Dre was honing his inner Muhammad Ali energy.

"You see that ninety-six Impala in *TREALTV*? We used to race that car, and Mac Dre wanted to buy it. Me and Dre went racing on Highway 80, and he got me by a little bit. After that race, he kept asking me, 'What you want for it? My car was supposed to beat yours, but I barely got you.'"

At the end of the race, Mac Dre pulled up next to B-Luv (who was filming from his car) and uttered what would later become one of his trademark slogans: "Thizz or Die."

CHAPTER NINE

THE BIRTH OF THIZZELLE WASHINGTON

Some of Mac Dre's most fun, most irreverent music was made in the early 2000s, as he began settling into his newfound freedom, prioritizing the party vibes of the turn of the century and attempting to shake off the trauma of prison life and street struggles. Through his gregarious personality, Mac Dre returned to the rap world with a mission that was always much bigger than him: he wanted his record label, Thizz Entertainment, to become a viable avenue for his close friends and family to make some money, to finally escape the generational poverty that had plagued so many in The Crest. He wanted to be more than a mere beacon of hope—he wanted to be the one to create an empire big enough to save everyone in the neighborhood.

In 2000, Mac Dre released *Heart of a Gangsta, Mind of a Hustla, Tongue of a Pimp*, an eleven-song offering produced by Outbac Records, which is owned by James Ross and now does business as EHustle Entertainment. In an interview with Ghetto Celebrities, Mac Dre says Ross never paid him for the release and distribution of the album. The experience of relying on others to move his music likely influenced Mac Dre's decision to start his own label and go the independent route. *Heart of a Gangsta, Mind of a Hustla, Tongue of a Pimp* was nonetheless another classic Mac Dre album, featuring "Hy Phy" with Keak Da Sneak and PSD and the standout track "Don't Be a Punk" produced by No Face Phantom. The cover features a typo (there's no "A" in "Heart of a Gangster") and shows Mac Dre in a bulletproof vest with his chains still on. The typo and the mixtape themes cover only add to the mystique surrounding this early release, which acts as a great introduction to the creative direction Mac Dre veered into in the coming years.

His fifth studio album, *Mac Dre's The Name*, came out on June 13th, 2001, and features an appearance from Daz Dillinger, a Snoop Dogg affiliate from The Dogg Pound who shows up on the album's final song, "Dangerous," with Bad Azz. This record finds Mac Dre in decidedly darker form, burrowing into the disorienting rat race of attempting to outrun the federal government while trying to make enough money to put food on the table. "Be About Your Doe" featuring Cognito is perhaps the best song on the record, with a slowed down, relaxed beat that Mac Dre approaches with pimp-like ease, choosing to basically just talk slick over the production and worry about rhyming cadence later. Some of Mac Dre's best songs are like this, with his charisma and natural gift of gab taking center stage over any actual raps. It's a formula also used by East Coast rap titan Jay-Z, who's known for not writing down his lyrics before entering the booth to record. Mac Dre shares some of this same genius, being able to use his natural storytelling abilities to carry a track.

The first true classic to be released by Mac Dre in the 2000s, though, was easily *It's Not What You Say . . . It's How You Say It,* which came out in November 2001. This is the album where Dre truly found his sound in the post-prison years, with futuristic and crisp production quality worthy of the greatest rapper in Bay Area history. While this is by no means a perfect record, it's an important one in the way that it catapults Mac Dre's regional sensibilities into something that could be played around the entire nation. Both "Have You Eva" featuring Dee and Little Bruce and "Always Inta Somethin'" are certified Mac Dre classics. The latter features a show-stealing verse from J. Diggs, who was arrested with Mac Dre and served a decade at FCI Lompoc for conspiracy to rob a bank. This verse basically acted as a reintroduction to Diggs, who would go on to become CEO of Thizz Entertainment in the years after Mac Dre's death.

Mac Dre's way of embracing an affinity for high powers and supernatural auras was enticing to new and old fans alike.

The cover for *It's Not What You Say . . . It's How You Say It* features Mac Dre himself, fitted in a white Kangol and bandana draped over his head with sweats, a T-shirt, and a jacket, moving left to right eleven times. As the first Mac Dre figure arises from an old school Mercury Cougar, he begins to fade and then reappear as he heads into a red Range Rover. The clever cover showcases Mac Dre's drive to better himself and his status in the world, using the vehicle as his proverbial mode of transport.

The album also boasted a few features with Little Bruce, with whom Mac Dre had briefly feuded in 1990. Little Bruce was affiliated with E-40's Sick Wid It Records and had released a well-received debut album in the 1990s before leaving the rap game to focus on pimping. He was well connected in the local sex trade and was making hand over fist without ever having to enter the recording studio. It wasn't until his former enemy, Mac Dre, returned from prison that he was convinced to give music another try. According to an interview from 2006, Little Bruce said it was a run-in with Mac Dre in Las Vegas that finally convinced him to begin rapping again.

"I was standing on the strip at a liquor store, and I heard, 'Punya! Punya!' I turned around, and there's Mac Dre right there in a big-ass Excursion," Little Bruce says. "He pulled over, and it was on from then. We hooked up in Vegas, we took over the Crazy Horse, we took over the Spearmint Rhino, Cheetah's. We were in every single studio! We did it big. We went to every casino gamblin', just having a ball. I'd fly to the Bay and check on his house, he'd fly to the Bay and check out my house. When we got cool like that, that's when he started asking me, 'What you wanna do? I'm finna start this Death Row-like shit.'"

Little Bruce remembered Mac Dre already having grand plans to turn Thizz Entertainment into a powerhouse like Suge Knight and Tupac Shakur had turned Death Row into the behemoth it was years earlier. Little Bruce and Mac Dre exploited their former feud for their collab, "Chevs and Fords," which pits the two rappers against each other once again (Mac Dre being the Chevrolet fan and Little Bruce being the Ford appreciator). In a Bay Area culture that values impromptu car meets and sideshows, this song is considered an anthem in the same realm as "Sideshow" by Traxamillion. Little Bruce's friendship with Mac Dre would only continue to blossom in the following years, with Little Bruce even choosing Mac Dre and Thizz Entertainment to release his next album.

"Thizz brought me back into the entertainment world; Mac Dre did," Little Bruce says. "My arch enemy in rap, and even though our neighborhoods were funkin', he embraced me. And then I gave him my independent album, *Give It to Me Baby*, which he put some new songs on and turned into 'Mac Dre Presents.' Muthafuckas was shocked by that."

While Mac Dre was beginning to hone his craft with a series of mature, career-defining albums, he was also busy recording material for *TREALTV*, which had cameras following him around 24/7. It's some of the best footage of Mac Dre still available and shows him at a time of his life where he was perhaps the most productive. It was around this time that he began adopting a litany of nicknames and pseudonyms, including but not limited to: Thizzelle Washington, Al Boo Boo, Ronald Dregan, Pill Clinton, Judge Dre Mathis, Mac Drizzle, Mac Drevious, The Furly Ghost, The Genie of the Lamp, The Make it Happen Cap'n, and The Thizzard of Oz. Each identity seemed to be more than a funny name, with Mac Dre presenting the ability to morph into numerous characters using different voices and speech patterns. He was a true entertainer in every sense of the word.

He released his *Thizzelle Washington* in August 2002, featuring a tie-dyed and hippie-themed cover that matched the lightness and humor of the record. It's the seventh full-length album from Mac Dre, and it produced one of his most timeless songs. "Thizz Dance" is a Bay Area classic, but that honestly feels like a limiting description. Partiers on the West Coast had been taking ecstasy, the street name for MDMA, for years by this point. The drug first appeared in the United States and Europe in the 1980s. It was mostly associated with club drugs like cocaine and speed—anything used to help people stay up and party for longer.

In 1985, as part of the war on drugs, the United States outlawed MDMA under the Controlled Substances Act as a Schedule 1 drug, like marijuana, LSD, and heroin (meaning it had a high potential for abuse and no real medicinal value). However, the ban didn't do much to slow its popularity as a club drug in the US. In the late 1990s, Mac Dre and his crew helped popularize MDMA to a new community separate from rave culture, introducing the drug to hip-hop fans and residents of The Crest. The psychedelic aspects of MDMA helped to change the entire mood surrounding Thizz Entertainment. Mac

Dre began rapping about other psychedelics, like mushrooms and LSD, and it was clear his mind was being expanded by these substances. His music began transforming into something altogether more fun and lighthearted, while also remaining close to the streets that birthed him.

"Thizz Dance" encapsulates Mac Dre's knack for trend-setting slang and culture-defining dance moves. It introduced the word "Thizz" into the lexicon, which is allegedly the noise an ecstasy pill makes when it's dropped into a drink for consumption. The most recognizable dance form of this era is called the "Squawking Eagle," which Mac Dre does in the video, making a gigantic frowny face like he "smells some piss" and flapping his long arms like a bird of prey. Other songs on *Thizzelle Washington* also capture the fun nature of this time, including "Boss Tycoon" and "Dollalalala Lotsa Paypa."

It was a period of prolific output for Mac Dre. Most of the music he recorded in his more than two-decade career was between 2000 and 2004. In 2002, he released *Mac Dre Presents: The Rompalation III*, which consisted of nearly 20 posse cuts and makes for a nice showcase of what would become the Thizz Entertainment roster. His next solo release, *Al Boo Boo*, came out in 2003 and is considered Mac Dre's best album by a small legion of fans. It's the sunniest—and perhaps funniest—Mac Dre album in existence. The title itself is a reference to shitting, the idea being that he's shitting on any rap competition in Northern California. The beat for "Genie of the Lamp" is almost goofy-sounding at first listen. But Mac Dre is easily able to match its absurdity with raps and voices that felt captured while he was in the middle of getting hammered on vacation. This album could have been recorded in the month after or before his famed trip to Hawaii, as documented on *TREALTV.*

"Something You Should Know" and "Mafioso" are also stand-out tracks from *Al Boo Boo.* Records like these capture Mac Dre's singular humor and overall vision for the future better than most. The beats were getting better and more fine-tuned for him specifically, with producers being able to bring out his signature personality with ease. Mac Dre was also earning a name for himself as someone who's willing to collaborate and build up younger artists. This is perhaps why it's almost impossible to listen to all of Mac Dre's music. He recorded so much, and with so many artists, that it's hard to catalog everything he's done. No matter how long you've been a fan, it's still possible to discover a new Mac Dre verse or an unreleased song you've never heard.

Mac Dre was also beginning to venture out past his Northern California comfort zone. He was gaining significant fan bases in Oregon, Washington state, Los Angeles, Las Vegas, and Kansas City, among others. His penchant for creating club bangers with a special Bay Area twist was becoming known around the country, and it really felt like the Thizz movement was beginning to sweep the nation. He did all of this while starting a label and preparing to release two albums on the exact same day.

Kilo Curt remembers arguing with Mac Dre over which album to release first, *Ronald Dregan: Dreganomics* or *The Genie of the Lamp.* Mac Dre wanted *Genie,* and Kilo wanted *Dreganomics.*

"It didn't matter; they both hit the indie Billboard immediately," Kilo says. "Our edge was to keep pumping Mac Dre out there—we didn't wanna keep our fans waiting."

Dreganomics and *The Genie of the Lamp* seem like sister albums in many ways. They could have been released as a double album but dropping them separately was easily the smart move. It's some of Mac Dre's best work, with many of his top singles to this day having appeared on one of these two records. They came out on July 20th, 2004, just fifteen days after his thirty-fourth birthday. On the cover of *Genie*, Mac Dre is dressed like an old prophet in Eastern Indian garb.

Genie is the darker of the two records, with Mac Dre saddling in for an excitedly sinister approach to relationships and partying. His pimp archetype is on full display with songs like "Make You Mine" and the Suga Free-assisted "My Alphabets," which sees Mac Dre holding his own next to one of the most successful pimp/rappers in the game. While *Genie* has its comically dark moments, it also has some of Dre's most accessible tunes, including "Not My Job" and "She Neva Seen." Both songs show him improving at making the kind of rap songs that have true crossover appeal: songs with easily quotable choruses and crisp Bay Area production.

Dreganomics, on the other hand, is perhaps Mac Dre's most radio-friendly album to date. That's not to say he sacrifices his artistic worldview for larger audiences—it's more that his party-fueled, street-smart raps were finally finding production worthy of the artist, as Mac Dre fully matured into the next phase of his career.

"Feelin' Myself" is perhaps Mac Dre's biggest song to date and has been cemented as a certified Bay Area classic. There's not a house party you can attend in the Oakland and San Francisco area that won't be playing it at some point in the night. It's so iconic, crowds can often be heard rapping the entire first verse without missing a word.

> "I'm out of this world, not your run of the mill'n.
>
> My name is Furl, I'm the owner of the building.
>
> I'm a stoner and I'm chilling with two bitches like Jack.
>
> I pimps and I mac drive a Benz and a 'Lac.
>
> Man, I've been in the back with the groupies and the stars.
>
> I've been out front with the thugs in the cars.
>
> I've been on the yard with the Mexican mafia.
>
> And I only run with niggas that'll kill and die for ya.
>
> I'm popular, I'm a rap star.
>
> But I live like a rock star running from the cop cars.
>
> I drop bars wit slaps that knock hard.
>
> And I charge with this dick extra large.
>
> I'm sicker than SARS, higher than Mars.
>
> And I treat my bitch like an ATM card."

"Feelin' Myself" became such a big song that Nicki Minaj and Beyonce made their own collaborative version, loosely paying homage to the original, in 2014. This newer version ended up spending more than twenty weeks on the Billboard Hot 100, making it the longest charting non-single by a female rapper. This is one of many examples of Mac Dre being decidedly ahead of his time. He made the type of free-wheeling rap music that would come to dominate hip-hop culture in the late 2000s and early 2010s. "Feelin' Myself" is also the Mac Dre song that is most associated with "Hyphy," a brand of turn-up music that he and other Bay Area mainstays helped to popularize.

Even though Keak Da Sneak came up with hyphy back in 1994, the movement didn't have its moment until 2006, when E-40 dropped his pivotal album *My Ghetto Report Card*, spawning the mainstream radio hit "Tell Me When to Go," featuring Keak. The movement was defined by its parties, referred to as "sideshows" by those in the know, wearing stunna shades, and ghost riding the whip—a dangerous and highly criticized act in which the driver puts a car in neutral and dances alongside or on top of it as it rolls. All this on top of its particular musical style: anthems with BPMs cranked high. In an interview with *Complex* from 2016, E-40 said that hyphy is a certain feeling.

"Hyphy is energy. Hyphy is a lifestyle," he says. "It originated with the streets. I credit people like Keak Da Sneak, Mac Dre, and plenty more. It's really a way of life, just hard-headed and really energized, like, 'He just a young hyphy dude,' or 'Man, he hella hyphy.'"

Bay Area legend Mistah F.A.B. agreed on the origins of hyphy music when asked in the same interview, saying, "It was Mac Dre and Keak Da Sneak. You have to say those two in unison. Dre was a fascinating man. In this world today, someone becomes far greater in their past than they are in their present. Mac Dre was already huge. And this is before he went to jail. So, when he came out and reinvented himself to become Thizzelle Washington, he became even huger. When he died, his reputation went crazy. Through it all, Keak

Da Sneak was there. Keak Da Sneak has transcended a few generations of Bay Area music. And he's still here."

Mac Dre's former manager, Stretch, told *Complex* that people weren't aware of the complexity of the movement until they saw it with their own eyes in Mac Dre's *TREALTV* series.

"Everything that people associated with hyphy, from ghost riding to stunna glasses and all the cliché stuff, was first seen in Mac Dre's *TREALTV* DVDs," he says. "That put a face on it when people weren't even seeing sideshows. They weren't seeing any of those things. And then from there, after *TREALTV* came out, all these other DVDs like *Oakland Gone Wild* started coming out."

Producer Rick Rock likes to describe the music side of hyphy as high energy, big bass lines and some pivotal Bay Area elements.

"It's an energy that touches your chakras, your energy sources. Things that automatically make you feel great, and you don't know why," he told *Complex* in 2016. "Hyphy was a great time when we had our own sound signature. The world was like, 'That's theirs.' We couldn't describe it; we knew it when we heard it. I know I could sit down and make one at any time. I start at a certain tempo and give you a certain feel with the frequency itself. The emotion was in that frequency, how I go up and down with the chord range. I'm doing it in that frequency that makes you say, 'What is that?'"

Although hyphy music didn't take off until a few years after Mac Dre passed, his later catalog has nonetheless become synonymous with the movement, further cementing Mac Dre's name in history and proving that he really was years ahead of his time. Songs like "Get Stupid," "Thizz Dance," and "Feelin' Myself" will forever be considered canon to the hyphy genre, as will the various *TREALTV* tapes that showed the visual aspects of the lifestyle for the first time. Hyphy music would later be mimicked and expanded upon by the South with "Crunk" music—a brand of club-friendly rap that shares much in common with hyphy. Crunk music would reach heights that the regional hyphy sound never quite did after Lil Jon and The East Side Boyz went number two on the Billboard Hot 100 with "Get Low" featuring the Ying Yang Twins.

Setting up recording spaces in various parts of Northern California was more than just a business opportunity. It was also Mac Dre's way of providing a spiritual space for brotherhood and bonding where growth and creative kinship could be facilitated. Mac Dre paved a way for artists like Mistah Fab and the Mob Figaz to embrace their quirks and eccentricities, which became the ultimate musical and artistic nirvana for them and others. Mac Dre himself was heavily influenced by Oakland's Gregory Jacobs, known by his stage names Shock G/Humpty Hump. The same year that Mac Dre won the Hogan High talent show, Oakland-based Digital Underground recorded one of the highest-selling records to ever emerge from Northern California with "The Humpty Dance," recorded not far from Vallejo, at Starlight Sound in Richmond, California.

"The Humpty Dance" was released to radio, causing a frenzy across the nation, and was later followed by a music video that featured the double-edged persona of Shock G and his alter ego, Humpty Hump. In the video, Shock G appears as both personas on a stage while adoring fans dance and scream along. Driven coincidentally by a sample of Sly and The Family Stone's "Sing a Simple Song" with its long drum loop, "The Humpty Dance" eventually sold over one million records and helped to launch Digital Underground into super-stardom. "The Humpty Dance" is Shock G's second song to feature his alter ego "Humpty Hump," who debuted on "Doowutchyalike," which was Digital Underground's first video release in 1989.

Mac Dre and Humpty Hump, specifically in "The Humpty Dance" and "Thizz Dance," used incredibly playful lyrics to create traditional dance rap songs. Humpty's use of silly lines about "I'm spunky / I like my oatmeal lumpy," resemble lines in Mac Dre's "Thizz Dance" where he instructs listeners on how to get involved.

"First, I do like this.

Put a look on my face like I smelled some piss.

Bounce to the beat till it starts to hurt.

Then I dust all the smirk off me shirt."

While Mac Dre's directions and Shock's parody bars are different, the themes are very much alike. Later, in "The Humpty Dance," Shock G delivers a ridiculous four bar jolt:

"I get stupid.

I shoot an arrow like Cupid.

I use a word that don't mean nothing.

Like looptid"

Shock's use of the word "stupid" in 1990 is later a catchphrase and ideology revisited by Mac Dre again and again, including with his album "Stoopid Doo Doo Dumb" and the incredibly popular 2004 record, "Get Stupid." Shock was the first to call for folks to get stupid, which generally meant wild, fun, carefree, and rambunctious. A similar four-bar flow from "Thizz Dance" pays homage to the satirical predecessor that is "The Humpty Dance":

"Now I'm slugged up.

And diamond grillin' it.

I don't care who I'm in the building with.

I do the dance with Nancy Von Chillinwich."

In 2003, Mac Dre appeared on Turf Talk's album—his first appearance on E-40's Sick Wid It label. According to his interview with Doxx of *Strivin'* magazine, Mac Dre says he got a call from E-40 about the collaboration.

"Charlie Hu$tle (E-40) asked me to get on a song with him. We've been on the phone, I'm waiting for Charlie Hu$tle to give me that call to drive up to the studio, then me and him are gonna get down."

Five weeks before his death, Mac Dre gave one of his last interviews. He laid out his plans to release new music at breakneck speed.

When asked what his next move was, the smiling MC responded, "Some ideas just pop into my head. I buy a lot of cars; I do a lot of driving. So, when I'm driving, things just pop into my head. You have to jump on your ideas immediately, and that's what I do. Whether it's recording a song, an album cover, a video, a new concept I'm coming with at a concert, show tape or something. I just don't hesitate. BAM! I'm using that! The next theme, I'm glad you asked me because me and my Cuddy, Mac Mall, hooked up. We are doing an album, the name of it is 'The U.S. Open.' I'm Andre Macassi and he's Mall Macenroe. We played tennis with the mic."

With the beef between Mac Dre and his protegee Mac Mall squashed and several new projects in the works, Mac Dre looked toward a bright future.

"My objective is to keep the fans stimulated. Keep them on me. Once they get bored, they get on someone else, and you're not hot to them anymore. I'm really trying to represent for this soil on a world-wide level. So, people in Japan know we have dope rappers in the Bay that ride around in fancy cars."

IN HIS OWN WORDS: THE LAST INTERVIEW

Originally appeared in the film *"The Gift,"* Recorded in 2004.

Interviewer: What is rap?

Mac Dre: What is rap? That's a good first question. Rap is a way of expressing yourself through words on top of a beat, whether it's a certain frame of mind you might be in, or want to be in, or experience you might have had. There's many ways you can express yourself. Those are your styles.

Can anybody rap? I mean, can anybody be a rapper?

I used to ask myself that all the time. When I came home in '96, I tried to actually make a rapper out of anybody and nobody, and let me tell you: not everybody can be a rapper. Unless you have enough money to force feed the public. To make them believe and to dress him up. And then you can make a rapper, but he won't really want to be a rapper. He probably won't last long. One-hit wonders. You can make a one-hit wonder if you got enough money.

What is it you like about rap? Is it the beat or the lyrics?

Right now, times are changing. When I first started, it was more of a combination of both. When I first started listening to rap, it was Sugarhill Gang and Curtis Blow. It was a combination of both lyrics and beats wrapped together was everything. Then times changed.

Groups like Public Enemy came out, and lyrical content really became more of a factor. People wanted to hear what you were saying if you're really saying something; if you're not saying nothing, we don't want to hear it. But nowadays, the beat is like 95 percent of what's going on. You could be saying anything as long as it's a banging, slapping beat. You can get the hot heads banging, you feel me? It's a slap!

What is it for you?

Right now? It's always lyrics for me. It's always lyrics, because I don't just rap for the fans on the street. I rap for the rappers that rap, too. I rap for Yukmouth, and Keak (Da Sneak) raps for me, and we rap to each other. So, I'm always going to be lyrically tight because I'm rapping for my niggas too! I can't have any faults in my game. So, it's basically a lyrical thing, but I gotta pick the right beats to get the right people to listen to it. You can't just rap over what you want to rap over all the time. You gotta pick beats to where people want to listen.

Most people might think you make records just for the fans, but you also rap for your homeboys and the people you came up with, your peers. Is there like a fraternity of rappers? Like, do you see Dr. Dre around?

I ain't met Dre yet. There's certain levels. It's like AAA baseball—they're still pros, but they haven't made it to the real pros yet. The people who are pros are all-stars. There's just certain levels, and I treat everybody who's giving it a certain effort with the same respect. Once you reach certain plateaus, it really becomes about record sales. That's what they respect: the record sales. Once you gain notoriety and your sales go up, that's when you get to the next professional level. I still ain't made it to the top plateau yet; I'm still reaching to get up there with people like Jay-Z and them. People like Tupac, who

I've been following for a long time. Me and Tupac used to do shows around here back when it was really rap. I did five years and all, but we were really rapping.

What's going through your head when you're on stage?

Shit, it's beautiful. When somebody from a total opposite walk of life is sitting in front of me singing my lyrics word for word, just vibing, feeling it, knowing what I'm saying even when I'm using slang words I might have made up that day, but they know by the way I used it in a phrase or whatever. This is someone who's nothing like me, not color, the way we dress, the curls in our hair. Yet, he's sitting right in front of me, going word for word. That's what it's about right there baby. And after the show's over, the promoter comes and cashes me out my bread.

It's like you're communicating?

It's definitely communication! For me, I'm representing a secret society of people that I know the rest of the world doesn't even know exist. It's just as entertaining as the rest of the people that's actually on TV. There's a whole culture that I'm representing. So, I'm communicating with, and for, the people and that culture. Showing them something that they might not otherwise be exposed to hearing.

What do you feel is the influence of pimping on the MC?

That's a good question. Pimping has a lot of influence on the MC because it's all about a pimp's mouthpiece. Some of these strippers and hoes these days are bad, beautiful, they could be doing modeling or whatever. So, for a pimp with a dime or a dollar in his pocket to get this girl to turn over her everyday earnings, which can range from $500 to $5,000 a night, and do it on a consistent basis with four or five of them? You got to come up with some of the most catchy things that a girl ever heard. So, when a pimp talks, a rapper listens— he's listening to this man, saying, "These are words I've never even heard put together; I haven't even heard the president talk like this." So, it's just those one-liners that keep the people interested. The pimp does influence the rap game.

What is a pimp?

You got people that define the word "pimp" with a few definitions, but the real, hardcore meaning of pimp? From around here in Frisco, where pimps are originally from, like Fillmore Slim and them? A pimp is a man that's getting his money. His business is making these women go to work and make money and whoopty whoop, as well as managing their money. He's running a business off of sex, a lady selling sex. Sometimes they don't even have to sell sex. I know women out there who make five Gs just for going on a shopping spree with rich people. Just buying jewelry for the weekend for five Gs. Bitches can get on an airplane for five Gs just to be with a rich ass guy for a weekend. Just so he can show off at the parties and shit. He wants a tight ass, blue-eyed, blonde-haired bimbo with him.

What's the difference between a pimp, a player, a gigolo, and a mac?

Pimps are structured. They have rules, morals, standards, and codes they go by, and they're real serious about their business. It's a real business with a pimp.

A player is just how it sounds. He's playing! He's got lines of bitches. He's doing what it takes. He's a player, he's good at it, and he's in the game. A player is a person who really plays the game.

A gigolo? You know what that is. That's a dude who likes to fuck, and he gets paid for it at the same time. Whether it's a welfare check or not, he's still getting paid. He's keeping it sharp by fucking these top-notch ladies that want to cheat on their husbands or what have you. I know a few guys who are working their gigolo game. Clean cut in Italian cut clothes, with those tight silk shirts and black, shiny shoes, or what have you. You gotta have the stamina though.

What about a mac?

Well, my name happens to be Mac Dre, and I got two definitions for that. "Mac," that stands for "mastered the art of communication." Like you said, this rap shit is about communication, and I got my bachelor's in this communicating game, right? With all races, or even kids, you feel me?

The other mac, like Too Short and them, is a form of pimp, but he is more lenient with his. With pimps, there's rules and it's structured. A woman could get slapped by her pimp. A mac will more so do what he wants to do. He's still pimping, but he's doing it the way he wants to do it.

What is it about the pimping that attracts females?

I'm exposing a game right now, and pimps might not want me to get too deep into this on camera, but a pimp is articulate—they can talk, and they know more things than the average black guy would know. It fascinates these women to be around a real nigga. When they peep the realness, it's an infatuation. Then most girls, when they run into that money at a young age like 19 or 18, cannot manage their money for nothing in the world. They can act like they're going to save up and get a Mercedes, but then they won't ever get the Mercedes. A pimp is going to make sure his bitches are buttered, got money, got cars and anything else. Because the more buttered they are, the better they look, and the prices go up. So, they're going to get treated good. It's like a baby on a titty thing, you need it for a minute, but some people get strung out on it. They become dependent. A pimp becomes like a guardian. Someone that can handle their business better than they can.

A lifeline.

If I have a pimp, I don't have to worry about bills or someone beating on me. He got it all.

Who are you? Who is Mac Dre?

I'm many people, and they all want to get paid. I've been a lot of places, and there's no place like The Bay because so many races interact with each other, and they get along good. There's not a lot of racial tension out here. Any tension comes from "he's from here and he's from here" or "she said this, or she said that."

I was born in Oakland. I was raised in Vallejo, Concord, San Rafael, Marin County, everywhere, you feel me? And I've kicked it with all different types of people. Sometimes I get tired of being thugged out, so I go kick it with the other guys, whoopty whoop. So, I'm many people, and I think that's what made my style so different from everybody else's. I got Asian cats, my Filipino niggas, my niggas in Frisco, Mexicans. A little bit of everything. I got all kinds of friends.

Talk about the value of that.

It's so valuable, because you can do things that other people can't because they have their blinders on, they haven't opened up and actually learned. If they have been exposed to the stuff, they weren't learning and seeing what's real. I'm a people person, and I'm interested to see how other people live and what they might be doing. When I went to the feds in Lompoc, I had to be aware of my surroundings, and I had to have a good judge of character within the first two or three minutes of meeting somebody, because something can go down within the next five minutes, you feel me? You gotta be knowing what kind of person you're dealing with. I got a good judgment of character while being there. Plus, the feds is not like the state pen—you got people from all fifty-two states and the other areas the United States has, like the Virgin Islands. You got mob people, you got Jamaicans. So, I'm in there interacting with all these people, and they want to hear me rap because they heard I was a rapper. They heard I was nice on the street, and they got interested, just like I'm interested in them.

How did it feel being behind walls and having people know you? What was that like?

I was twenty-one years old when I went to Lompoc. You know how you hear stories when you're young about the penitentiary and people getting stabbed up. So, I didn't know what to expect. I wasn't scared, but I was prepared for the worst. When I got up in there, I was surprised by how many people from the Bay Area were there and knew about me. So, they were like, "Yeah, that's my partner," and I became the representative for our area's rap. I became the poster child, and every so often I'd have to go up in the band room and eat a rapper from New York, LA, wherever they came from, whoever thought they could rap. Their people would bring them up to the band room to see if they could get down with Mac Dre, you feel me? It gave me a little bit of respect when I was in there. I was up there with the mob figures as a mob figure, you feel me? Because I could entertain.

Were you born who you are, or were you taught to be what you are?

I was born in Oakland. Stayed in Oakland for a minute, then went back to Vallejo where my mother was born. So, I'm a Bay Area cat to the heart. Since before I can remember, my mom has always worked in Frisco, commuting to Frisco every day. Basically, I'm just like you or whoever else from the Bay Area who might be watching and is into rap music.

And who I am? I'm the Scarface of the Bay or Jay-Z. You know how every area has one? I'm the rap superstar of the Bay. I'm representing because the Bay Area wants to see people from the Bay Area on TV with fancy cars. I'm trying to be that guy for the real Bay Area folks, you feel me? That's why every time you see me, I'm going to be pulling up in something that costs $60,000 or $70,000 or better.

What was the crack era like?

It was just right up everyone's alley. So, everybody is doing the dope dealer thing at the same time, people are getting hooked on the drugs. So, it's affecting everything; even the people that don't smoke or do anything are getting affected, because it's changing the economy and everything. That was the biggest transition from when I was a little guy to now. When crack rocks hit? Nothing has ever hit like base rocks.

You can get major time selling crack. Why do you think people don't consider that? Why do they think about the money side more?

It's the get rich quick aspect of it. "Bam, I could go out here tonight and have $1,000 in my pocket. I don't have to worry about where I'm going to get the investment money or none of that. It's just quick money right now." So, the need for the money outweighs the risk, because when you need money to eat and survive, this is the quickest way some people know how to do it, you feel me? They're willing to take that risk because what else can you do sometimes? There are other things you can do, but that's how some people think.

Like you said, whole communities have changed and have been destroyed from crack, from this one drug that's different from all the other drugs. What's the worst thing about crack?

There's two worst things. The worst, worst thing is the lives it's destroyed and all the great people that could have been somebody smart. You got nerd crackheads that could have been rich or helped a lot of people. A lot of good people got fucked off by doing crack. Another bad thing was that a lot of people who were rich or ballers back in the day are nothing now. It's an illusion type of thing. You're on fantasy island for a minute! Because it's not there anymore.

Everyone that I looked up to is now calling me and asking how they can get into some legit money.

Is there anything good that came from crack?

Y'all wouldn't have Mac Dre! Probably Tupac wouldn't be rapping. A lot of people would not be rapping if it wasn't for the troop shoes. The niggas on the block slanging rocks. The 9mms, the Uzis—if it wasn't for all of that, rap wouldn't be as interesting, you feel me?

Some rappers say that the crack game created a hustle. It created a mentality, especially in the Bay Area.

It did. That's what a lot of people did. They applied their street hustle to the rap game, and it worked until the major labels started microscoping what was going on and muscling out the independent guys with a little bit of money with a lotta bit of money. They made it hard for the independent labels because they saw that we were making it hard for them. We had arrogant rappers out here who weren't signing. I still haven't signed yet. Why not? Because I make more money than you trying to offer me right now.

Nas is the originator of this quote, but it's been sampled by Biggie and Jay-Z. But it says, "sometimes the rap game reminds me of the crack game." What does he mean when he says that?

Honestly, most of the people at that level of rap came from the crack era. You're dealing with a lot of the same attitudes, temperaments, and mentalities that came from there. It's the same people but a different business. It reminds you . . . when someone is trying to work you on a rap deal, it'll kind of remind you of a cat arguing over a few grams, you feel me? Unless you're at the top where you're talking to executives. But you never really get away from talking to those kinds of people. You gotta always have muscle, because knuckleheads and cutthroats are going to always be in the business regardless.

When I say the word "respect," what comes to mind?

Respect is when a man can interact with people and not be tested beyond normal tests. You know how somebody might ask a question like "what do you do?" That's respectful compared to "what set are you from? Whoopty whoop." That's not respect. So, when you can have enough respect to where someone is not over-testing you? That's respect to me. Whether it's a business deal or you're at the restaurant ordering food. If somebody doesn't over-test you, that's respect.

What's the difference between laws and rules?

That's easy. A law you can go to jail for. A rule is just a rule. If you break the rule, you might get a penalty or something, but you ain't going to the big house. A law is more final than a rule.

In your world, what do you respect more?

The law! They made me respect the law, though. I respect the blood out the law. I'm going to figure out why they're messing with me and make sure they know I'm not that one. They make you respect it. I didn't at one time, but I give them their respect. I'm going to get out of your way.

Is there any difference to how respect was shown back in the day to how it is now?

A little, it's basically the same though. You see kids doing the same kinds of little tests we used to do—the same type of disrespecting—but it's more high-tech these days. Hate crimes, shooting at schools and shit, just to show off! Same shit we were doing, but it's just a little more 2005-ish now. We didn't have access to guns when I was in school.

Who do you think the police respect?

Each other. That's about it. Once you cross that line, it doesn't matter. They respect the chain of command too. Anybody that's above them as far as their chain of command. They don't respect anything else. They're jealous; it's just the mentality of the police. Some of them can contain it, some of them can't. But they respect each other.

What sets you apart from other MCs and rappers when you're at your best?

You come to a Mac Dre show and you can see any type of person there. That's what sets me apart from the rest of the rappers. I could have Friday, Saturday, Sunday shows lined up. You might go to the Friday show and see nothing but niggas. On Saturday it's nothing but white cats from college. On Sunday, it's all Eses, Mexicans. That's what made me how I am right now. I have all kinds of fans.

Do you enjoy that?

I love it! It's the best feeling in the world. Never limit your options.

How does being at your best influence the people around you? I mean the quality of person you are. How does that impact the people who depend on Dre?

A lot of the people I rap for or work with, I'm damn-near a carbon copy of them. We don't have a lot of people from where we're from, or not even from where we're from, but the type of person that I am, so when they see me doing it, they say "do your thing, man!" They succeed when I succeed.

How does that make you feel?

That's what I'm doing it for! I got people in Kansas City; I got people in Denver. I know what these types of people want, and they're not getting it. That's what I'm here for.

What is love?

Love is a strong liking of anything. A strong, strong liking. I love my car. I love my bitch. Don't touch my bitch, don't look at my bitch. Love is strong; you'll do anything for what you love. You can like somebody, but love is when you can't see yourself without them. When it hurts you to be without whatever it is that you love. It could be your dog or whatever. Your homie, your Cuddy, whatever it is. It's an inseparable bond.

What's the difference between love and loyalty?

These are on two different plateaus. There's a lot of people that I love who I know won't or can't be loyal. Loyalty is a trust thing. Love is in here. It's a feeling that you have for someone, you feel me?

You might love your cousin, but you know you can't loan him no money because you ain't gonna see it again!

Right, right.

Do you think a pimp could fall in love?

I think most if not all pimps are in love. How could you not be in love when a broad is giving you $1,500 a day? "Here daddy, I'll do anything for you!" You gotta love that! Pimps are in love with their hoes. They have to be!

You came up around a lot of different things. Hip-hop, rap, the dope game, bank robberies. Do you have children?

I have a daughter.

How would you feel about her getting involved in the game you've been exposed to?

That's another thing that I try to project in my rap. There's other ways to have fun rather than resorting to the illegal. I try to show that you can be smarter than having to resort to taking a chance or a risk for some money. I just try to show people another way to make money and have fun without putting yourself in harm's way, you feel me? I try to make them go another route. I rap about things that happen so they can see they don't want to do that. A *scared straight* kind of thing.

How old is your daughter?

Thirteen

You try to show them a different route?

I got partners who are dead. If you go for the quick broad, you might get set up. I give it to them straight! You don't want that to happen to you. I did that and it didn't feel good, I didn't like it. It wasn't right.

Would you say you're in love with money?

No, I'm not in love with money. I'll burn up a $100 bill right now. I spend money like it ain't shit. I disrespect money. But I know it's a necessity. I can't be a person who's like "I'm cool with a $7 or $13 an hour job, or whoopty whoop," That's not enough to feed the whole family, so you gotta have money! If it's a necessity like water, I'm trying to have as much of that as I can have.

Could a real hustler ever be broke?

Yes, because he could take a gamble, put all of his chips in two or three different things, and they all might go bad. But a real hustler is going to come back up—just give him some time.

Why is that?

A real hustler could go broke, but a real hustler can't stay broke. How long have you been hustling then? We're gonna have to take the "H" off hustler. You a "Ustler" now!

Describe the attitude necessary for someone to really get some paper. What is it about a hustler that makes it so he can't stay broke for long?

They realize it's a necessity and that things won't run right without the money coming in. Some people are content with being broke. Some people don't have a place to stay and are living couch to couch. A hustler is going to know it's a necessity to get that money to live right.

What's the worst thing about money?

The worst thing about money is that it can make people kill for it. There's hustlers so into hustling that they will take another life for some money.

So, money's not worth more than a life?

No, nothing is worth more than a life. That's it.

Do you think the war that's happening right now is any different? Are they killing for money?

Not everybody in that war is killing for money.

I mean the people that are sending them.

Not everybody who's sending them is killing for money. Some think they have a legitimate reason to fight. It could be a holy, spiritual, or religious cause. And some people are fighting on American soil for revenge. Or they're sending them over there just because of revenge. I don't think everybody is in it for the money. A lot of people are, though.

Why do you think money has inscribed on it, "In God We Trust?"

I think it started because we had to have it on there. We were representing God, but now I don't think people are really paying attention to "In God We Trust"; money is just money now. It doesn't have anything to do with God or nothing like that now. But I think it started off as a way for God to represent our goods and services. That's why there's a stamp on there! To remind us that money is not over God. But now, I think it's lost its meaning.

Has money become like a religion?

For religious people, money is business. Churches need money, that's the thing. Some people use religion to get money. I see a lot of people doing that.

Is that pimping?

Like a motherfucker!

Last question: Is money worth risking your life for? In the short or long run?

I'm the kind of person who can handle that risk. If you're a nerd with glasses who knows it's not their thing, they shouldn't be doing it. But if you can take that risk, sometimes you have to do it.

CHAPTER TEN
LEGEND OF THE BAY

Mac Dre's final album, *The Game Is Thick, Vol. 2*, was released only thirteen days before his murder. It's meant to be the spiritual successor of his mentor The Mac's first EP from 1988, *The Game is Thick*. The Mac's monumental EP is the quintessential Bay Area deep cut—a springboard that launched the pimp archetype that artists like Mac Dre, Too $hort, Suga Free, and E-40 would later expand on (and in some cases, perfect). Mac Dre had always looked up to The Mac and had never strayed from paying homage to his lost friend.

The album was released on October 16th, 2004, and featured multiple Mac Dres in various outfits handing a suitcase to one another in front of two parked cars. The album was decidedly harder than his party-themed releases from earlier in the year. It showed Mac Dre leaning into a pimp-like archetype that he'd often explored in previous albums.

Mac Dre is at his best in songs like "Retro Dance Record," produced by One Drop Scott. The production is pure hyphy, with bouncy synths and a simple bass line that Dre molds into his own with an onslaught of gut-busting one-liners and pimp-like swagger. "For you, I'd walk to Modesto," he says. "Big booty, shake it mommy, let's go!" He follows this up with a line about Christopher Columbus and the Venetian merchant and adventurer Marco Polo. It's an excellent example of Mac Dre's subtle humor and expansive worldliness that made him so accessible to fans outside of the Bay Area.

His last performance in the Bay Area was at San Francisco's illustrious Candlestick Park on the same day *The Game Is Thick, Vol. 2* was released. It was a near sold out event, and Mac Dre was riding off the release of his new album. His music seemed to be catching on to the masses, and he was looking forward to touring and sharing his act with the rest of the country. One of the places he was most excited about performing in was Kansas City, Missouri. The KC hip-hop scene and the Bay Area's hip-hop scene shared a mutual appreciation for each other's music. Artists from the Bay Area easily sold-out shows booked in Kansas City, and vice versa. In early October, Mac Dre had booked a show in Kansas City for Halloween weekend. It was scheduled for October 29th at the Kansas City National Guard Armory and was set to feature three of the Bay Area's biggest acts: Yukmouth, Keak Da Sneak, and Mac Dre.

Mac Dre and three friends flew from Sacramento to Kansas City, with a quick layover at LAX, on October 27th, 2004. He and his crew spent the next two days hanging out around the city and promoting the show. Mac Dre went to a record store signing on the day before the concert and was set to appear on a radio station, but he couldn't make it in time. Due to a series of unfortunate events (set off by an inexperienced concert promoter and a disorganized event plan), the Mac Dre, Keak Da Sneak, and Yukmouth show had to be shut down early. Keak Da Sneak and Yukmouth both decided to take flights back to the Bay Area the next day, but Mac Dre decided to stay back a few days longer for reasons unknown.

At some point, Dre agreed to do a club walk-through at the Atlantic Star on Halloween night. The Atlantic Star was a well-known club in Kansas City, and the expectation was that Mac Dre wouldn't even have to perform—all he had to do was make an appearance, drawing in patrons and boosting sales for the club. This event was allegedly organized by the same concert promoter that had set up the concert at the Kansas City Armory two nights before. It wasn't supposed to take all night, and Mac Dre left around 1:00 a.m.

At around 2:30 a.m., the white van Mac Dre was in was traveling northbound on Highway 71, just south of 75th Street, when a dark sedan pulled along the driver's side of the van and shot upwards of thirty bullets from two separate guns: an automatic rifle and a .45 pistol. The mysterious sedan violently rammed the driver's side of Dre's van in between taking shots. The driver of the van swerved off the road and into a ditch, tossing Mac Dre's body from the vehicle and onto the ground nearby. The driver escaped the crash and headed to the hotel, telling the front desk workers to call the police and that there'd been a terrible accident.

Mac Dre was pronounced dead at the scene. He'd been shot in the back of the neck and had been grazed by bullets in two other spots on his body. It seems hard to believe that Mac Dre could end up lying dead in a muddy ditch for more than an hour after crashing in such a violent way. More than thirty shots echoed in the night— and yet nobody heard or called anything in until the driver made it to the hotel. He died alone in Kansas City, thousands of miles away from his home in Sacramento . . . thousands of miles from the streets of Vallejo and San Francisco, where thousands of people still cling to his every word. It seems such an awful way to go for a larger-than-life personality like Mac Dre. A cosmic wrong that forever threw the world off balance for those who knew him best.

The KCPD have never arrested or charged anybody with the murder, and the high-profile nature of the killing has continued to generate rumors and theories among hip-hop fans and true crime aficionados.

A long-form article looking into Mac Dre's death was published by investigative journalist Donald Morrison in 2021 on the hip-hop blog *Passion of the Weiss*. The article uses more than 1,200 never-before-seen police files requested from the Kansas City Police Department to paint perhaps the clearest picture of what happened in Kansas City more than fifteen years ago. The gritty details are out there if you search hard enough, but the truth is that we'll likely never know the full story of what happened that night. What we do know is that Mac Dre's death became the catalyst for the deaths of at least three other people and was the beginning of a sordid tale of rap revenge and long-sought payback.

The streets began talking in the weeks and months after the death of Mac Dre. A local Kansas City rapper named Fat Tone was rumored to have been involved in the killing. Numerous sources were saying that Fat Tone felt disrespected by Mac Dre on the night of the show after he didn't invite the Kansas City rapper on stage during his set. The rumor was that Fat Tone killed Mac Dre to get back at him.

Fat Tone wasn't your typical gangster rapper. He actually seemed to live the life he rapped about. A few years before the Mac Dre killing, Fat Tone had narrowly escaped life in prison after multiple witnesses dropped out of a case accusing him of the double homicide of a nineteen-year-old girl and her unborn child. He served nine months in jail before the charges were dismissed. Fat Tone did little to stop the rumors of his menace. His image as a violent gangster helped him sell records, which is ironic, considering that music was probably one of the few hustles helping Fat Tone escape a life of crime.

And his music was good. His brash, violent, and honest take on Midwest hip-hop captured the ears of his Bay Area contemporaries in a way other Kansas City rappers hadn't. Mac Dre and Suga Wolf recorded a song with him for his 2002 album, *Only in Killa City*, titled "Cut Throatz." They were friends—and they stayed in touch enough for Fat Tone to know that Mac Dre was coming to town for Halloween weekend.

According to police files obtained by Morrison, multiple witnesses say they saw Fat Tone arguing with Mac Dre over stage time at the National Guard Armory show on October 29th. In fact, dozens of tips recorded by the KCPD feature some variation of Fat Tone and Mac Dre getting into an altercation. However, numerous witness statements say this never happened, and police were never able to confirm it.

Fat Tone and his lawyer met up with KCPD detectives on November 16th and denied any involvement in the murder, while acknowledging that he'd heard the rumors about his alleged involvement, according to Morrison's story. Fat Tone told them that every time something like this happens, he gets blamed, and that he isn't worried because he knows he did nothing wrong.

Fat Tone said he'd hung out with Mac Dre and friends at a hotel the day after they arrived in Kansas City. He'd also been to the show at the Armory and remembered Mac Dre briefly inviting him on stage. Several months later, Fat Tone would release a song where he denied having any involvement in Mac Dre's killing. But rumors persisted that Fat Tone actually released a song admitting to the crime—although it's never been found.

"Fat Tone had a reputation," Kansas City activist Alonzo Washington told Morrison in his investigation. "It wasn't like he was the greatest rapper in town, but he would be getting into a lot of trouble with the law, and so he had this sort of edgy thing with his music. He used Mac Dre's name to get a little more street cred for his career. But I don't think he did it."

In an interview with Kansas City's *The Pitch* from 2005, KCPD detective Everett Babcock said that he's convinced that Fat Tone did not kill Mac Dre. However, that didn't stop Fat Tone from facing deadly consequences over the unfounded rumors, and on May 23rd, 2005, seven months after Mac Dre's killing, Fat Tone and his friend, Jermaine Aikens, were murdered in Las Vegas in what is widely believed to have been retaliation for Mac Dre's death.

For many of Mac Dre's friends and family, the gritty details surrounding his death felt inconsequential in comparison to the deep loss they experienced due to his absence.

Dackeia Simmons recalls the last time she encountered her old friend, "Vallejo was so vast and special—so is Mac Dre," Simmons says. "The last time I saw Andre, I was home from Howard University. I was walking down the street, and I said, 'Andre!' and he said, 'What's up, Keyia? What's up, college girl?' I said, 'You're famous?' He said, 'Yeah, I'm famous.' This was on Stanford Drive. He was driving through with his big afro flowing and his big smile beaming. He pulled his star card on me but let me tell you that Andre Hicks was a nice young man."

The media rarely represents the man side of Mac Dre. They never come close to explaining the nuanced nature of his character.

He was a man who could never be defined or limited by his circumstances. Mac Dre was a rap star who funded children's programs in Sacramento, who did free concerts at Vallejo's Community Center near the Country Club Crest, and who helped support his friends in their many creative endeavors. Mac Dre handed out turkeys during Thanksgiving in the neighborhood that brought him up.

"Mac Dre treated us like equals," Kilo Curt says. "He was never just Mac Dre to us."

Nucci, a road manager and close friend of Mac Dre's, remembers him as a pioneer. "Mac Dre was more than a rapper," Nucci said. "He was an entertainer in the greatest sense. He was part MC Hammer, part Humpty Hump. He was fully Mac Dre. The man was world class."

Thizz Entertainment was left in dire straits in the months following Mac Dre's death. The Hyphy Hero's most commercially successful albums had been released on the independent label, including *Ronald Dregan: Dreganomics, The Genie of the Lamp, Thizzelle Washington,* and *Mac Dre's the Name.* These are all timeless records that will continue to be played for decades to come, but Mac Dre's untimely death created a leadership vacuum that threatened the existence of the label.

It was in the years following the creation of Thizz Entertainment that Andre Hicks gained a diverse new following, selling thousands of CDs in places like France, South Africa, and even rural parts of the United States. The label name helped further popularize the word "thizz," transforming the tone of the local hip-hop scene from hard and gangster to more wild, fun, and carefree.

The hyphy movement felt reinvigorated for a brief period after Mac Dre's death. This tends to happen in the wake of an artist's passing; people who never publicly showed love in the past all of a sudden claim to be day-one fans. Others who never bothered to listen to Mac Dre, or who had simply never heard of him, became curious about the music after hearing of the shooting. Tattoos, decals, shirts, and more bearing his likeness proliferated. Long-time friends and associates swore to keep his name alive. J. Diggs began wearing a gigantic "Mac Dre" chain around his neck, and Miami The Most began driving a black Hummer with his face on the side.

Thizz Entertainment immediately pivoted. The label's leaders accelerated plans to spin off the distribution arm, Thizz Nation. Mac Wanda took control of Thizz Entertainment as a way of controlling his large musical catalog, and overnight, Thizz Entertainment transformed from an active record label to the estate of Mac Dre. But it didn't prove to be that simple. Former close friends of Mac Dre's, as well as other loosely connected artists and Thizz Entertainment hangers-on, began to exaggerate their relationship with Mac Dre in the wake of his death.

Artists began using the famous Thizz Entertainment watermark in an attempt to associate themselves with the label under the guise that they were merely paying homage. It likely wasn't all malicious—Mac Dre had touched so many lives that people from The Crest and the Bay Area at large wanted to pay their respects any way they could. To outsiders, it became confusing trying to figure out who was officially connected to the record label and who was merely trying to capitalize off the Thizz Entertainment name. This became even more concerning when numerous former Mac Dre associates were named in a large drug trafficking case accusing over two dozen people of selling ecstasy and other drugs, including heroin, across Northern California and the country.

However, the actual owner of the label, Mac Wanda, and close associates like Kilo Curt and Ray Luv have never faced any criminal prosecution and were all extremely surprised that the label's name was even mentioned in case files and the news surrounding the arrests.

For nearly a decade now, during his birthday month, Mac Dre's fans, family, and supporters gather for a concert in his honor entitled "Dre Day," conceptualized by Wanda, Kilo Curt, and Ray Luv. Dre Day has featured everyone from Oakland's Kamiyah to legendary producer and hype man Lil Jon of Atlanta. Lil Jon's adoration for Mac Dre moved the Southern fixture to produce and record a song, using a posthumous verse from Mac Dre. With 2019's "Ain't No Tellin'," Lil Jon cranks out a bouncy, bass-heavy track where he gives love and respect to Mac Dre's region and to the slain rapper himself.

Perhaps one of the most iconic Dre Days was in 2018, held in San Francisco at The Regency Ballroom on July 5th—what would have been Mac Dre's forty-eighth birthday. It was hosted by Mally Mall and San Francisco radio station KMEL's DJ Amen and featured performances by Tyga, Nef The Pharaoh, Mistah F.A.B., Philthy Rich, Coolio Da Unda Dogg, and Baby Bash, among others.

Thizz Entertainment released the documentary *Legend of the Bay*, narrated by rapper and journalist Sway Calloway, in 2015. The documentary included never-before-seen concert footage, home movies, and exclusive interviews with Mac Dre's friends, family, and artists such as Wiz Khalifa, Tech N9ne, and Warren G. It's a documentary steeped in familial love and adoration. You can tell Mac Wanda played a large role in the making of the film, with an unconditional love for Mac Dre present in nearly every scene. The movie manages to not only be a love letter to Mac Dre and his legacy, but to the whole hyphy scene that he helped pioneer.

Ray Luv says of Wanda, "It's been almost twenty years since we lost Dre, and Wanda has been exceptional in keeping him alive. Wanda has done amazing work to have outreach to the younger community, especially with 'Dre Day.' A lot of the younger, newer artists were very much connected to Dre. He's one of the most named-dropped artists in the game maybe ever. He was so connected on a human level to people."

As "Young Black Brotha" the record label ascended, so did Ray Luv. His long-standing admiration and respect for Mac Dre, the man who gave the label its name and much of its identity, is as strong as ever.

"You had several independent Black people, and it wasn't just males. We had a lot of women who put Young Black Brotha together. It was all about doing it for myself. Music we barely sampled. It was created by young black people. It was about young black males and their lives. We talked about police brutality. Hey, Richard Pryor talked about it on stage, but we talked about it in a way to affect the young black brothas in the community. We didn't only make street music, we made good music—and Mac Dre was the king."

The list of rap entertainers and supersized personalities aiming to emulate and pay homage to Mac Dre are innumerable. From his colleagues J. Diggs, Dubee, Boss Hog, and Mac Mall to contemporaries E-40 and Lil Bruce, Ray Luv believes Mac Dre's legacy is everlasting.

"The whole goal in Los Angeles, for example, is to be synonymous with culture, and Dre is synonymous with Bay Area rap culture," Ray Luv says. "He's not a mascot, but he is the banner flying for the entire Bay Area culture. The people hold up the memory and image of Mac Dre."

Today, Mac Dre's name and spirit are evoked in countless songs every year. His influence can be seen in regional rap scenes across the West Coast, from the off-kilter and woozy raps of contemporary Bay Area rappers like Nef The Pharaoh and EBK Jaaybo to the mumbled, "nervous rap" popularized by Drakeo The Ruler and 03 Greedo in LA. Even Mac Dre's documentary project, TREALTV, proved to be far ahead of its time, with social media and concert vlogs proving to be more important than ever for artists wanting to connect with their fans. Mac Dre's legacy can even be felt when Steph Curry is knocking down a three pointer while giving his best "Thizz Face" to ESPN cameras.

Mac Dre will forever be known as the leader of hyphy and Vallejo's "Hometown Hero"—the rap pioneer who ensured that The Crest is known worldwide. He was the vessel through which thousands of people from the Bay Area's lived experiences were spoken. His music still inspires countless young Black men today. It inspires them to be the best and most fulfilled versions of themselves, to live beautifully and without restriction the way Mac Dre did all those years ago.

ANDRE LOUIS HICKS

JULY 5, 1970 – NOVEMBER 1, 2004

LIFE'S A BITCH

WRITTEN BY MAC DRE

It's not often young niggas get a chance to enjoy riches in legitimate fashion.

So many of us say fuck it get a bucket and run up in something and keep smashing.

It's all about survival but jealous rivals make it hard for us to do this.

So everybody got a gun but when we was younger our only weapon was our two fists.

Now who missed the first lesson in life don't be no punk.

If you a man have heart be a savage whether you sober or drunk.

I seen niggas in the pen getting their ass dug out over some hop or a pack of Camels.

But that's the game home boy and every move you make is a gamble.

Them squares don't understand so it takes niggas like me to explain it.

I show vengeance violence and hatred because underneath it's so much pain.

I ain't no sissy or punk so don't trip when you see me crying.

A nigga just hella mad his partners is dead and his folks keep on dying.

My enemies feel the same way they want me dead they think I'm the nigga.

That put they partner 6 feet under and left his son with no father figure.

I live day by day not giving a fuck and when they ask me why.

I pause for a minute then I reply because life's a bitch and then you die.

(Chorus)

Life's a bitch then you die.

Nigga don't want a whole slice just let me taste the pie.

They sent me to the pen for five years for a crime that was never committed.

I ain't no bank robber but that five years had me thinking maybe I should have did it.

Did my thoughts deceive me what a mutherfucker supposed to think.

Locked down trapped looking at four walls a toilet bowl and a sink.

Ain't that a bitch I've been struggling ever since I could remember.

But I stay strong year round from January all the way to December.

See I am a hustler I need cash bad as a fat bitch need jogging.

So I specialize in three things and that's pimping hogging and dogging.

Half these suckers walking around here fake as three dollar bills.

If you with that bullshit don't come around me I do this for reals not for thrills.

I got to watch my back for them suckers that's out to do harm.

Got a tattoo of a list full a partners that's dead that run all the way down my arm.

So if you see me mugging tripping and bugging don't stop and ask me why.

A nigga just hella mad because life's a bitch and then you die.

(Chorus)

I got a crew full of the realest that's deep as the Pittsburgh Steelers.

Retired bank robbers ex-dope dealers and adversary killers.

Our mission is simple get rich and stay real nigga.

So our kids can live fat better than we did when we was little niggas.

Life is short you only live once and ain't no telling when
your leaving.

So I'm going to do it all have a ball while I'm still living
and breathing.

See I am a philosopher and my philosophy is this.

Don't be no punk young homey if it's worth it take that risk.

Anything's possible but nothings for sure.

Got to take advantage of all opportunities and get your money
you know.

Love those who love you but don't never let it fuck up your vision.

How much love did your loved ones have when you was broke or
doing time in prison.

Stay on your toes don't fuck with hoes before you read them.

Watch your back for them rats that set niggas up to keep
they freedom.

It takes 365 days for the earth to spin one time.

But it only takes one minute for that guilty verdict when that snitch
drops that dime.

A damn shame I thought rat heads get nothing but cheddar.

But I got partners doing all day with 35 next to that letter.

So I'm in trouble unless I bubble so I struggle to keep my peace.

Staying money motivated with thoughts of Mike Robinson and
D.J. Cee.